A LIBERATING LIFE FROM SILENCE

DALE M. MARSH

A Liberating Life from Silence

Published by:
WinePress Publishing
PO Box 1406
Mukilteo, WA 98275

Cover by **DENHAM**DESIGN, Everett, WA

Printed in the United States of America

ISBN 1-57921-041-4
Library of Congress Catalog Card Number: 97-61157

Contents

Introduction xii

Chapter One
The Basic Foundation and Power in Growth 11

Chapter Two
The Conceptualization of the Holy Spirit, God's Kingdom and Faith 29

Chapter Three
Educational Synthesis as an Interpretation. 49

Conclusion 87

Agenda of Personal Theology

Addendum I
Wake Up to the Bible! 91

Addendum II
The Kingdom of God and Heaven 101

Addendum III
A Theology of Christian Faith 149

Addendum IV
A Theology on Divine Love 172

Addendum V
A Theological Approach to Power and the Holy Spirit . 198

Addendum VI
A Theological, Sociological and Psychological
Look at Divorce 206

Addendum VII
My Ministry as a Chaplain 221

Notes 232

Bibliography 236

Acknowledgements

Credit must be given to Dr. Daniel P. Fuller for teaching me how to understand the purpose for "generating principles"; Dr. George Eldon Ladd for teaching biblical theology; Dr. James E. Loder for giving me the language to explain and defend my answers about learning skills; and to Dr. Millard R. Shaull for opening my soul and mind to the theology of liberation. These men were my professors at Fuller Theological Seminary, Pasadena, California, and at Princeton Theological Seminary, Princeton, New Jersey.

Dr. Fuller taught his students how the one generating principle in any writing can be found. A book entitled How to Read a Book, by Mortimer J. Adler, and the Bible were Dr. Fuller's primary sources.

Dr. Ladd taught his students about the kingdom of God from biblical theology. I only hope I can clearly interpret his incredible insights.

Dr. Loder required all his students to write a paper of his recommendation for the following outline:

1) The basic foundation and power for growth.
2) The conceptualization of the Holy Spirit.
3) Educational synthesis as an interpretation.

Dr. Shaull taught all his students how a person can be liberated from the depth of his or her soul, and how to breakdown their walls of suppression and oppression for the freedom to speak out.

I am forever reaching out for and holding on to my faith in God's grace and mercy, that I shall always learn more. –Author

Introduction

My book is written to encourage other people with learning deficits. God remains ready to transform lives into a more meaningful and challenging life of learning. All the walls that engulf victims are only needing to be broken down to free those victims from the suppression and oppression that's within the soul. My wall was silence, which only I was able to breakdown. I want to share how this was accomplished.

God is revealing His nature in us through times and situations that are designed to change all of our innermost parts (Proverbs 20:20–27; 2 Corinthians 4:16–18). God's active nature is seen in His Spirit—the Holy Spirit.

God's active nature changed my life. The time of day could have been morning when the school's academic advisor explained why my aptitude scores were too low for entering college. She discouraged me from even applying. All students were advised of their aptitude scores during the close of their junior year in high school. I have no strong memory of how I felt or responded to the bad news. I can recall her logic that my parents' blue-collar employment along with their education could have a bearing on my own aptitude for higher learning. Many people who heard this story found it almost impossible to believe. I will never forget her comment, and I view it as a time and situation that God revealed His nature in my life. Some place in my innermost parts was my natural learning ability. This only had to burst out of my mind like a volcanic explosion—from silence to an explosive and liberating life. However, it took another twenty-two years before my liberation was ever completed.

Learning for me was a struggle. My boyhood could be described as life under the lower socioeconomic standard—with insufficient time for studies and parental encouragement. The academic advisor was correct about my parents' education level and their employment; she did not know about my dad's alcohol abuse and infrequent employment. My parents also had no ability to empower proper learning skills. Our family income was from my dad's infrequent employment, my mother's employment and newspaper routes that my brother and I had. Our economic survival was a higher priority than my education.

My educational performance was below average from kindergarten through the fifth grade. I always passed from one grade to the next on probation and developed very few learning skills. I recall my paternal uncle's comment that he had never met a child before me who could not speak clearly. I spoke with little or no organizational thought in my sentences. I somehow began to develop a few learning skills beyond the sixth grade. I passed these grades and people began to understand my speech more from that time on.

The junior and senior high school levels were difficult for me. My obligations with three paper routes and the chores at home did not afford me time for homework. And yet, I did excel in algebra and art class. My fear to express my thoughts in the classroom only further prevented personal growth. Other students, who knew all the answers and could clearly defend their arguments, would somehow intimidate me from speaking out.

My conclusion will be a brief explanation of the kingdom of God, Christian faith, and divine love. The purpose is to promote a more definitive theological understanding of these themes. They also represent a theology I brought to my ministry as a chaplain in the US Army and the Department of Veterans Affairs.

During my ministry, I wrote sermons and lectures that represent my actual presentations. It was for the reason of sharing my work that these sermons and lectures were compiled to form addenda I through VII.

Chapter One

The Basic Foundation and Power in Growth

A dysfunctional family—with a frequently unemployed, alcoholic husband/dad and a dominant wife/mother responding as the "rescuer" for the family—is a condition which has a negative impact on children. I lived under this condition, which became the unsteady foundation and power for my spiritual, emotional and educational growth.

My elementary education up through the fifth grade was a bad start. I could only pass from one grade to the next under probation. I did not focus on learning while living in this dysfunctional family environment. I was not only suppressed from learning, but I also had poor speaking skills. In 1959, my dad's youngest brother told me that he had never before heard a child with such poor speech skills. He said my thoughts were not internally organized to make any sense for the listener. He also had no idea how to help me learn these skills.

Problems, such as I have just described, weren't discussed in dysfunctional families, and the education system didn't deal with them either. No one made the connection in ways that are being done today. Most likely, I was not the only child suffering from a deficit of learning skills. There were other dysfunctional families. A good conclusion is as follows: A child's basic foundation and power to grow must be nurtured just after birth and during the elementary grades. That same child must receive all possible guidance, support and love, and should live in a family free from dysfunctional disorders.

My brother and I suffered under such conditions that were only worsened by frequent moves—seven times during eighteen years. I managed to complete high school, but my brother only completed the eighth grade. My brother did complete a high school diploma through the GED, while serving in the US Army. There is no blame intended, but I hope to demonstrate how the unsteady foundations in my life directly corresponded to my future educational growth.

My parent's marriage, as previously stated, suffered from my dad's drinking problem and frequent unemployment. His behavior created frustrations for my mother and emotional stress for my brother and I. We had two fires in the house because Dad fell asleep while drinking and smoking in his chair.

Dad occasionally told me about his love for music and all the professional experiences he had prior to his marriage. He began at the age of three playing the "bones." He had a natural talent for them and eventually played the drums. Unfortunately, once he was the legal age, he did not turn down offers for beer from people who appreciated his talent. The offers continued even during the first year or two of his marriage. My mother could not cope with Dad's weakness since it always led to his absence from home and very little money to pay bills.

He quit playing professionally and tried to begin another vocation; he became a spindle sander for a furniture company. This was better than getting a divorce, but the change did not cure his drinking habit. He could not control his need for alcohol and losing a job always followed. I never believed quitting the band was his only failure since he also quit junior high school. Both failures affected my dad. Together, they became the kernel out of which all conflicts between him and my mother sprouted.

My mother developed a dominant personality from her defensive role and became the "rescuer" of the family. When my brother and I came of age, we got paper routes to earn money. I had three. These finances became part of the family's total income, along with the job my mother had to secure. Our family's income was never sufficient, but we survived.

My brother managed to complete most of the requirements in junior high school before the principal allowed him to quit school. I graduated from high school within the upper 25 percent of my class. I eventually came to the conclusion that my family background had contributed to my learning deficit, but only I can accept the responsibility for improving my skills.

My dad always said that the shame I felt from my elementary-school difficulties gave me the incentive to improve. I must agree, since I did improve and eventually passed. I also recall trying to cram an entire semester's course into a weekend before a high school final exam. I never found time to keep up with all my courses since I had the paper routes and chores to do at home. I felt shame from my low grades in these exams as well.

A few teachers tried to help me, but I still had difficulty understanding how one communicated by writing and speaking. This trouble followed me for many years—even after seminary. I seldom participated in class discussions since other student's scholastic abilities intimidated me. Those teachers must have felt there was power for educational growth hiding inside me. They are to be commended; both Proverbs 20:20–27 and 2 Corinthians 4:16–18 support this notion. I shall always be grateful to every teacher who gave any sympathetic help.

However, sometime during my junior year in high school, the academic advisor summoned for me to see her one morning. She said that in light of my recent aptitude test, I was not college material and should consider a vocation that didn't require a degree. Most people do not believe this story. I do not remember the immediate impact of her advice, but my response in later years shows a very strong impact.

Forty years later, writing this account of my educational development, I can look at five degrees hanging on my wall. I will repeat the comment from my dad: This negative advice gave me the incentive to face the challenge of college work. With this incentive and my stubborn character, I somehow doggedly completed five degrees. I continued suffering in shame from bad grades, and professors expressed doubts about my ability to graduate. For every hour most students spent studying, I studied for three hours; and I actually had doubts about myself on a few occasions. I experienced all of this, but I also experienced a powerful educational growth. I encourage anyone who feels waylaid by intimidation to enter college, to ignore it and go for it.

God is forever revealing His nature in us through hard times and difficult situations in order that He might change all of our innermost parts. God even works through teachers and other such professional people to achieve this change. He most definitely did this in my life.

My thoughts about the power in educational growth are not complete unless I conclude with a comment about my faith. I did not take my Christian faith seriously until I was in the eleventh grade and met a girl who attended a church where salvation was the primary focus. I did not understand this term, salvation, but I eventually learned it.

I recall going to the altar to repent during a revival the church had one week. Subsequent to that date, the power of my spirituality began to emerge during the summer of 1955. Jesus took on a new meaning for me, and I thank God for it. I slowly learned how the divine power of Jesus could empower my life. I cannot learn anything myself unless He, who is with and in me, empowers me to learn. Jesus is central to all I learned.

US Army Enlistment

Our foundation for power in growth is not limited to our educational experience; we also learn outside the classroom—at home, work, recreation, or any other place where the concepts and theories for learning can be encouraged.

Rich learning experiences took place during my time in the US Army. My total enlistment was for three years active duty and three years inactive reserve. I was sworn in as a private on July 12, 1956. I recall asking myself how I ever got into this crazy mess on my second day of active duty. Life was almost intolerable during basic training. I only had myself to thank or blame, and my Lord was the only source of power to help me continue with what I chose to do. I recall always singing: “Keep on believing, for God will answer prayers.” I understand these words are not exactly the same as in the song, but they are what I sang and what drove out my tent partner one night. It was my prayer for a hope of surviving military life.

As time marched onward, I continued to march through basic training. Once basic training was completed, I continued on with advanced training in cartographic drafting. This took eleven weeks and, upon completion with the lowest grade level, I was sent to Tokyo, Japan, and assigned to the 34th Engineer Battalion.

Enlistment did not include a college education, but I still learned about life's good and bad elements from discussions with people. I regret that I had little incentive to take any of the available courses being offered on the military post, but I also accept it as my own choice. A few of the soldiers who were drafted were educators. They taught me so many practical things. I shall not forget their concern and their willingness to share their knowledge.

Military life in the mid-‘50s offered me three aspects of education through experience—courtship, human relationships and spiritual insight.

The Aspect of Courtship

A “Dear John” letter from my high-school girlfriend came within the first few months I was in Japan. I learned about pain from this sudden separation, and how healing comes at a later date. I had friends to offer their support while I began to heal. A common supportive remark was, "Cheer up, there are plenty of other fish out there." This gave me strength to face other girls. These friends, who were soldiers and missionaries, introduced me to four girls whom I recall. One of them became my wife.

A soldier in Japan did not date a decent girl since there was a social pressure against it. I began to learn how to protect reputations. I would only meet with these girls at church or at other functions. I never regretted following these rules of conduct in Japan. I always felt they were better than allowing any decent girl to suffer through a social stigma. This cautious approach was not normal for me, but I soon accepted it as a reality for that age. My friends who also understood this social pressure always gave me support. I confided in them about my personal feelings toward the young lady who later became my wife in Grand Rapids, Michigan. My courtship in Japan was a good learning experience and foundation for future relationships.

The Aspect of Human Relationships

Human relationships are valuable laboratories for learning about life. They introduce such virtues as obedience, steadfast commitment and strong self-confidence. Jesus, in the New Testament, is a good example of these virtues and how to apply them in any relationship with people.

I had numerous discussions for hours with my peers in the army about life and the nature of people. A few were college graduates and they enjoyed such discussions. I struggled with personality traits of being overly sympathetic, subjective, dominant or hostile. How did the virtues make any sense with these traits? My greatest help came from comparisons between military life, with rules to obey, and life in general. Military life nurtures obedience, commitment and self-confidence. And yet, each person will choose to what extent he or she will be obedient, committed and self-confident.

There is no doubt in my mind that those discussions and relationships with my peers in the army had a positive affect on my life today. They broadened my interest to learn. Also, I did not know how or why this experience occurred, but I enjoyed it until the time to explore it further came during my studies at Princeton Theological Seminary.

Credit for broadening my soul and mind and increasing my foundation for growth power is given to Dr. Daniel P. Fuller, Dr. George Eldon Ladd, Dr. James E. Loder and Dr. Millard R. Shaull—professors at Fuller and Princeton Theological Seminaries. Their wisdom and love for teaching caught my attention. Together, we finally got it together, as some would say. The Holy Spirit worked through these men to open up all channels in my innermost parts of soul and mind. It was like a volcano erupting with all sorts of information for me to retain. No, I did not become a genius; I did feel like expressing myself more freely. I felt free to speak out. I felt the same way when I was still in Japan learning a great deal about human relationships.

Soldiers say a lot about their first sergeants. I was no different. All soldiers must admit that they were good teachers, just like my four professors. I respect them for giving us the greatest lesson of all: how to survive in war. Yes, first sergeants brought out the animal within us, but that was one of the most important factors for survival. We had to learn how to use it properly and never to harm the innocent. Credit must also be given to first sergeants for teaching obedience, steadfast commitment and positive self-confidence. Such factors ensure that all soldiers will find success in their complex military relationships.

These factors somehow became a part of our total being. For example: my buddies and I enjoyed exciting discussions about being committed to our weekend training in the summer of 1958. We were also learning obedience. The location was close to Mt. Fuji, Japan. We carefully planned what we would do as team members in our unit. We then carried it out. I learned the importance of commitment and obedience when I realized our lives were at risk if I chose not to be committed to the "game plan."

This same sense of commitment and obedience remains with me today. I shall remain committed and obedient forever. Somehow the warnings from an old master sergeant at Fort Hood, Texas, where I took my basic training in the summer of 1955, came alive in the innermost parts when I later had training in 1958.

Our first sergeant had a unique way of teaching us self-confidence. We were required to stand for an inspection in guard mount. The preparation was incredible. Our uniforms had to be heavily starched, we had blocked neck scarves, and our boots and helmet liners were highly polished. He drilled us on questions he thought the inspecting officer would ask. One guard would be chosen as the best in the group.

The first sergeant only wanted his men to win. If we did not, then he brought shame on us. If we won, then we felt a great deal of self-confidence. He did not allow us to dress alone or sit before the inspection; another soldier had to assist. I cannot help but believe this kind of preparation remains with me today. Even on hot days, I always wear my suit when visiting patients in the hospital. Patients often asked me why. My answer is, "You deserve the very best I can give you."

Two important factors should be in one's value system: moral standards and tolerance. They rank very high in the military for soldiers of all grades. Although the army enforces high moral standards and tolerance, there are many soldiers who practice very little of either. I was not at all comfortable witnessing enlisted soldiers and officers stealing from the supply room or watching a battalion commander not tolerate the personality of a particular 2nd lieutenant. These soldiers were able to evade punishment in these cases only because they were not caught; and I feared my own future if I had "blown the whistle." The first example mentioned occurred when I was enlisted (1956–1959) and the second occurred when I was a chaplain (1972–1982). I am not proud of this action to remain silent, nor am I proud of a system that failed to protect the whistle blowers. Survival training came in handy at this point.

In later years, I learned from educators that relationships, in the army or otherwise, are an educational process with positive results. They foster self-confidence in older students who decide to attend college. I certainly went beyond the counselor's guidance from South High School.

The Aspect of Spiritual Insight

Any soldier can be appropriately tempered with spiritual insight. Any religious organization, such as a community church, will offer spiritual insight. One must choose the percentage of commitment he or she will have for these insights. This is especially true for moral conduct such as celibacy while the husband and wife are separated because of a hardship tour of duty. A soldier must decide whether to be 100 percent committed or less than 100 percent. The matter becomes tough whenever a soldier receives numerous temptations from community prostitution, peer pressure from military buddies, getting bad news from home, etc. A soldier soon learns that there is no flexibility for moral conduct.

Most churches teach against drinking for the protection of the body. Military regulations prohibit soldiers from allowing alcohol to reduce their high level of performance while on duty. And yet, soldiers received an incredible amount of temptation to drink, especially from 1950s through 1970s.

The NCO and Officer's Club constantly claimed they would go out of business if soldiers did not drink. Commanding officers mandated their soldiers to support these clubs by drinking, and the buddy system brought on pressure as well. Now these soldiers are being treated for substance abuse at our VA Medical Centers. How can the Veterans Affairs refuse treatment when this history is so well known?

I learned that a soldier could only commit 100 percent to drinking or 100 percent to sobriety. There was absolutely no flexibility for middle ground. A soldier's career could either excel by drinking in the club or be totally destroyed. The margin between the two was absolutely too narrow for even the strongest person to delineate. I chose to be 100 percent sober and sought the necessary spiritual support by attending chapel and post activities, visiting missions, and taking sightseeing trips.

As for chaplains, John gave me his friendship and practical spiritual guidance that meant so much to me. I later asked him to recommend me for the army chaplaincy in 1967—nine years after I knew him in Japan. His role as a chaplain had an incredible amount of influence on me, and he knew the young lady in the choir who eventually became my bride on August 27, 1960.

Among all the missionaries I knew, Stanley and Mabel were perhaps the most supportive of me. Stan even conducted our worship services on post after chaplains were no longer assigned to our unit. We also had a priest to conduct mass prior to the Protestant worship service.

Our unit was without a chaplain for two months before our battalion commander assigned me as his clerk of spiritual activities. My selection was directly related to my reputation of being a strong Christian, but it never sunk in until my buddies confirmed it one night.

After being assigned in August 1958, my first task was to locate Protestant and Catholic missionaries. This mission was accomplished, but I do not recall how. Stan was the Protestant missionary; I can't remember the priest's name. I was happier during this period than all the prior months in the army. This experience, as well as being valuably educational, influenced me to become a chaplain.

Marriage, College and Vocation

Approximately three months after I returned home from Japan and separated from active duty on June 9, 1959, I wrote a letter proposing marriage to the young lady in our chapel choir in Japan: Miss Yoko Yamashita. We only saw each other in Japan when we had chapel activities or when attending the same activities at the missions. We knew the same missionaries. I asked an army buddy of mine, Dick, whom Yoko also knew, to assist her. He and a mutual missionary friend of ours convinced Yoko that I was actually proposing to her. She did not want to accept. But after about three weeks praying and reading the Scriptures, Yoko finally received an answer from God to accept.

Her conviction that God was involved was confirmed six months after she came to America on June 19, 1960. She apparently had tuberculosis before coming, but four doctors never detected it during her screening. The illness became worse in January 1961 when Yoko acquired urticaria (hives) and a high fever. The doctor was amazed when he viewed her x-rays from Japan. The TB cavity was visible on her chest x-ray, and this doctor claimed it was only God's work that got Yoko to America. No one was allowed in the United States with TB during that period. She was then admitted to the Sunshine TB Sanitarium, Grand Rapids, Michigan, for the next eleven months. One third of her lung was removed in major surgery.

Our foundation for powerful personal growth was tested. Our marriage got off on a rough start, but the separation due to illness became more positive for us than negative. It was not all smooth and cheerful; neither were the many months after Yoko's discharge from the hospital. Together, we learned to work on our foundation of growth power. No one else had the right to participate with us.

We decided that I should move to Chicago, find work and remain there until Yoko could join me. Eventually, when we were financially able, I would attend an art college so I could teach art. The weather was too rough for Yoko, so her doctor recommended moving to California. I was able to earn credits during one semester at Chicago City College before the move to Long Beach, California. In this city, I attended both the City College and University at the same time. It was during my senior year at California State University when I decided to change from becoming an art teacher to becoming a US Army chaplain.

I entered Fuller Theological Seminary in Pasadena, California, in August 1967 to fulfill my calling for the chaplaincy. Although there weren't any interruptions between my studies at the city college, state university and the seminary, a short period as a pastor at the Mira Loma Church of God and one more year of graduate work for my masters of divinity from Anderson School of Theology was essential before I was ordered to active duty as a US Army chaplain on July 8, 1972.

Classes

I am one person who experienced a sense of hardship with a learning deficit, and I do not know how many others like myself experienced similar hardships. My only purpose for writing these observations is to encourage the others out there to accept the challenge of college life. The balance of this chapter will therefore share more observations and lessons from my undergraduate and graduate studies. Chapter 2 and 3 will make little sense without this background and experience—where I came from, what potential I had for learning, how I learned what power I did have and when I was able to grow.

A Typical Large Class of Students

All my classes in college and seminary never had below twenty-five students. They always ranged from forty-five to one hundred. Very little student involvement with the teacher and individual ideological expression could ever occur with a large class; especially for students with a learning deficit.

Large classes and students who were aggressive with their answers always intimidated me. I had barely begun my thought process on the teacher's question when another student would burst out the answer. Sometimes I knew the answer, but the class discussion was already on the third or fourth question that followed before I could decide how to answer. I felt my answer would seem unrelated and make little sense to other students and the teacher as well. On a few occasions, I tried to answer the teacher's question when the class was through with the subject. There was usually a fairly long silence before the teacher would avoid my answer altogether and continue with the subject at hand. I always felt crushed and hurt from this response. Many days would pass before I could get over the hurt.

I also remember those moments when it occurred while I taught for Anderson University and St. Leo College. I would repeat the question that my student wanted to answer, and then would reflect verbally on the answer. The whole class could then appreciate this student's incredible insight. This was a very good lesson to learn.

A Class with Lectures, Reading Material and Films

Lectures, reading material and films are excellent when used properly by both the instructor and the student. More is learned when class lectures highlight the important information and bring further insights to a subject—clarification of terms or philosophies and the introduction of recent research. These proved valuable for me since I could not totally conceptualize the lesson without these resources.

A typical textbook always seemed to lack a particular detail that I needed to fully understand an issue. I learned the value of these resources when I studied at Fuller Theological Seminary, but rarely used them in college.

A foolish young man was said to have driven his jeep into the depths of the jungle and thought that only a small pistol would be needed for his protection. In reality and from forgetfulness, he forgot that he stored a heavy firearm in the back seat. He was obviously foolish for assuming his small pistol was an equal match for the dangerous jungle, but also for forgetting about his heavy firearm. The story continues, but the portion that I shared will illustrate how I studied in college. It was not only foolish to think my class notes and textbooks were sufficient for making good grades, but also foolish that I did not use everything at my disposal—related books, films and video tapes from the library.

Fuller students were strongly urged to take the broader approach in their studies. I had to spend eighteen hours a day to fulfill that requirement.

A Class with Grade Competition

I cannot be even more naive than to admit that I was totally unaware that students were hiring an agency to prepare their term papers and take their exams. I even asked these students how I could do better, and they chose not to be honest with me but only advised to studying harder and taking better notes. I not only felt excluded because I was older than the average student, but I also felt they feared the possibility of my being an undercover agent for the college.

Did competition drive these students to take such drastic measures? High grades appeared more important than quality of knowledge. This weakness is carried over to the business world. Quantity and money are more important than the quality of service. People are rewarded well with a grade point average (GPA) of 4.0, or when a lab technician processes 100 DNA plates within 8 hours and when a medical specialist recoups 2–3 million dollars at a Veterans Affairs Medical Center. This whole issue creates an incredible moral and ethical challenge.

Today, grade point averages continue to be the number one topic of discussion between students and educators. It may not be resolved under the present method of measuring knowledge. Most people agree that present methods only produce negative results. I came to this conclusion after I became a victim. I recall a common warning: A student must earn a 3.0 GPA or above to avoid being labeled as a loser. I completed my undergraduate work with less than a 3.0 GPA. I not only wore the label of loser, but I also received the judgment of probation to study at Fuller Theological Seminary.

This issue of grades must be resolved in order to produce a par excellence quality of education.

A Class without Grades

My visit to Oxford College in England was quite a revelation. I asked one of the mentors about the grading system. He simply said they do not offer grades. Students are not advanced to the next level until they achieve a par excellence quality of education; grading A or F serves no productive purpose. Teachers can always use the percentage system to measure knowledge and to decide whether a student is ready for a higher level of education. A student can have an evaluation of highly successful or outstanding. What college or employer would ever refuse a student with this evaluation?

Personal experience and the educational system nurtured the quality of my education. I may have encountered good and evil from both, but I still achieved far more than my academic advisor in high school claimed I would—five degrees. There were several reasons for my achievement.

The first reason is stubbornness. I cannot say when I realized this, or even when I accepted it, but this became my positive means to learn. I knew giving up would never achieve anything. Poor grades caused shame, but they would not overcome me.

Second, I had faith in God and that the Holy Spirit would teach and guide me to all truths. I firmly believe only the Lord's help got me through all five colleges and seminaries.

My wife is another reason. She not only believed in me, but our Lord strengthened her to find work and earn sufficient money to pay for tuition, which made time for me to study.

The last reason is my hidden ability to actually learn. I came to the conclusion that all of God's children have the ability to learn. Some learn slower than others; some experience too many confrontations in life; and still others need encouragement to simply try.

Chapter Two

The Conceptualization of the Holy Spirit, God's Kingdom and Faith

The Holy Spirit revealed God's nature in my life. I am grateful for this blessing and for the revelation of my natural ability for learning. I was once silenced, but now I am proclaiming to you the gospel message—God's kingdom and faith.

Chapter 2 is devoted to three concepts and how they were responsible for my life's liberation from educational bondage.

God Became Man

Some of the various scripture verses on the subject of God becoming man are:

> Then God said, "Let us make man in our own image, after our likeness." (Genesis 1:26a)
>
> Then the Lord God formed man of dust from the ground, and breathed into his nostrils the breath of life. (2:7)
>
> Then the Lord said, "My spirit shall not abide in man for ever, for he is flesh…I will…destroy all flesh in which is the breath of life…." (6:3, 17)
>
> And behold, a young lion roared against [Samson]; and the spirit of the Lord came mightily upon him. (Judges 14:5–6a)
>
> …And Elizabeth was filled with the Holy Spirit. (Luke 1:41b)
>
> The Holy Spirit will come upon you [Mary], and the power of the Most High will overshadow you. (Luke 1:35)

These Scriptures represent God's nature being revealed to me through difficult times and situations and also represents my growth in educational abilities that liberated my life from silence.

The above scriptures tell of God's power to change at will a person's life and how to know life and death since God is the Alpha and Omega. They explain that God works through His Spirit and that we can experience His power. They emphasize the importance of growing in our faith and love since God is love. God demonstrated that love by sending His only begotten Son, Jesus, born by Mary. His one of many reasons for coming was to transform a person into something better than previously known. His divine mission was mandated under the divine authority of the kingdom of God.

The Apostle Paul was a great supporter of this notion: "Do not be conformed to this world, but be transformed by the renewing of your minds, so that you may discern what is the will of God; what is good and acceptable and perfect" (Romans 12:2). I therefore see no reason for any person to expect anything less than God's power and love.

God's nature was not always easy to understand after my spiritual conversion in 1955. I struggled twenty-two years for clarity. Although part of the process began while I was at Fuller Theological Seminary between 1967-1970, and Anderson School of Theology in 1971, the final came in 1977 at Princeton Theological Seminary where I learned the proper language to describe a conceptualization of His nature from Dr. James E. Loder. He taught theories on educational ministry, which I later used to develop my conceptualization. God's nature is learned primarily from a comparison between our human nature and Jesus as the Christ.

My justification of salvation is based on the four following points:

1. Biblical claims that Jesus is the Son of God (Matthew 3:17; 16:16; 17:5; Mark 1:11; Luke 9:35; John 1:34; 3:16)
2. We were created in the image / likeness of God (Genesis 1:26)
3. God's nature is revealed to His people (Luke 17:30; Romans 1:17–18; 2 Thessalonians 2:1–6)

4. We shall know God the Father by knowing His Son, Jesus (John 8:18–20)

In regards to conceptualizing God's nature, Dr. Loder developed a theory called cohesion and synthesis. The process essentially brings God's nature together with human nature and reveals a reflection of likeness between the two; i.e., the image of God (Genesis 1:26). Theologically, this theory visually conveys a message that Jesus not only became man but also extended Himself by giving His Spirit to us (Acts 1:5, 8; 2:33). The theory does not convey an absolute difference between God and human nature.

How can Jesus be both God and man? This phenomenon was too bizarre for many people during Jesus' ministry, and that has not changed for many people today. We cannot find the actual words *incarnation* or *incarnate* in the Bible. We only have strong language describing this concept, such as the following:

- Christ coming in the flesh (1 John 4:2; 2 John 7; Romans 8:3)
- Appearing in the flesh (1 Timothy 3:16)
- Christ introduced as the Word (John 1:1–5)
- And as the Son of God (Matthew 3:17, 16:16; John 1:34, 3:16)

God simply chose not to reveal how His Son became man while still God. Theologians say we are called to a faith that demands our belief that there is truth in this claim.

God knows that people will only see His greatness when the final product of Jesus is projected before the world. Many people may not consider this important, but it is true. Scripture commands us to believe that Jesus is God and divinely conceived by Mary. Also, the Almighty God is the Father of Jesus, not Joseph.

Each person needs to work out his or her own theory to explain this incredible phenomenon. The greatest problem is the limitation of the English language. A visual drawing usually communicates more clearly than words. Consider figure 1 for a possible representation of how to communicate Jesus as both human and God.

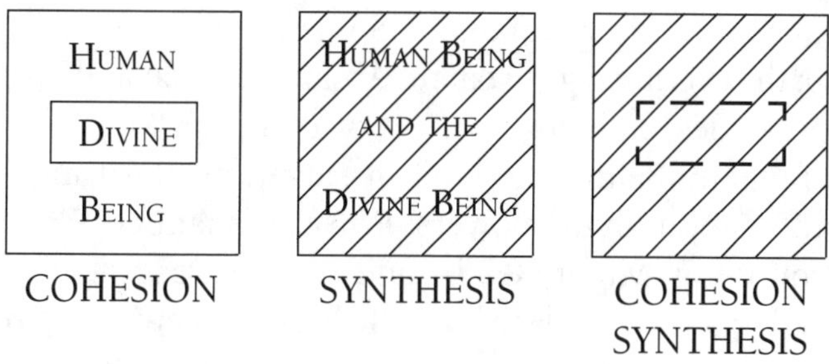

(fig. 1)

Jesus existed as God and man (synthesis) and served as God performing miracles (cohesion / synthesis). His spectacular illustration of this phenomenon is the miraculous resurrection of Lazarus (John 11:1–44). There is no human power known to science that has ever intercepted absolute death as Jesus did. Jesus simply commanded Lazarus to rise. His voice was the only connecting power with this miracle. Both the miracle and the incarnation of Jesus are unexplainable, but our faith calls us to believe in them as truth.

Figure 1 also shows how human beings operate under divine powers (cohesion). The Apostle Paul taught the importance of healing as a gift and that our Lord empowered us for such ministry (1 Corinthians 12:9, 28–30). A healing ministry is only one of the many gifts God gives to His people. One ought to seek appropriate training, but many examples are found in the four Gospels and the Book of Acts. I highly recommend a serious study of these New Testament books.

God's Redemptive History

The Old Testament is a logical beginning since it points to Jesus in the New Testament. Some of those concepts include: the everlasting covenant, Abraham's great and mighty nation of descendants, the Son of Man, the Messiah, the Superangelic Being, the God of salvation, the King, the Anointed with divine powers, Priest, Immanuel, Wonderful Counselor, Mighty God, and Prince of Peace.[†]

Perhaps the most striking of these concepts would be the superangelic/supernatural man called Jesus. It certainly characterized Jesus of Nazareth. His miracles were a paradigm strongly affirming the biblical and theological link between the Old and New Testament. But Jesus had to offer evidence. Whereas the Old Testament points to Jesus, He had to point back from the New Testament to explain Himself as the fulfillment of prophecy.

Unfortunately, God's people were looking for a second Davidic kingship in the Messiah—one who would restore them to an earthly rule. Jesus did not focus on such an earthly kingship, but rather a spiritual kingdom. Both Jesus and His cousin, John the Baptist, proclaimed it (Matthew 3:2; 4:17). Jesus said, "I must preach the good news of the kingdom of God to other cities also: for I was sent for this purpose" (Luke 4:43). Jesus spoke of the kingdom of Heaven more than the kingdom of God.

Listeners struggled with the process of understanding Jesus as the Son of God and one having reigning authority in God's kingdom. Jesus' disciples had difficulty with this message, and the Jewish leadership had enormous problems understanding it. The Jewish leadership was looking for God's redemptive plan to be played out in another Davidic kingship, Jesus knew God's plan would only unfold in the reigning kingdom of God. Theologically, Jesus and the Heavenly Father knew full well that human beings could never redeem themselves from original sin (Genesis 3:22–24). Jesus as the Son of God stepped in to be the Redeemer for the world. His death, victorious resurrection and ascension to His Heavenly Father are what offers the world eternal life with God. His forty days on earth prior to ascending gave proof that He always represented the truth. His mission now required further ministry by the Holy Spirit, which Jesus sent (Acts 1:8; 2:4).

We are still in the age of the Holy Spirit. He is the third personality of the Godhead—Father, Son and Holy Spirit. The Father's mission is recorded in the Old Testament, the Son's mission is recorded in the New Testament and the Holy Spirit's mission remains presently active. The Father's mission was to establish fellowship with people and offer an introduction of His Son as their Redeemer. Jesus' mission was to proclaim Himself as the Son of God, Redeemer and Messiah in the redemptive plan. The Holy Spirit's mission is to continue with Jesus' ministry.

We are now waiting for the Second Coming of Christ (Revelation 22:20). The Holy Spirit empowers all Christians with grace to endure hardship and pain, faith to trust in God always, love to accept and care for other people, and a forgiving heart. This is God's nature stretching out with His love and making contact with His people (Isaiah 14:26–27; Ezekiel 37:1–6).

The Godhead enjoys the reality of being loving and just. My personal conceptualization of this Godhead only has the mind-boggling English language for communication. With my learning deficit, it took many years of effort to understand the Godhead, and I went through various stages. These stages each represent a fresh start. I was given a fresh start in the public school system, during my enlistment in the US Army, during college and while attending seminary.

Symbols can be an appropriate way to communicate these fresh starts. I entitled such a new beginning as "The Dawn of a New Day." This theme initially came from Isaiah 42:9 and Revelation 21:5 that tell us: "[God] will make all things new." The word dawn clearly represents something new for the day. The birth of Jesus was the beginning of a new covenant relationship with God's people. His birth fulfilled the Old Testament Law by establishing Jesus as the final authority over the Law. The Old Testament church was reformed into the New Testament church with Jesus as the founder and head. It can be verified by His resurrection at the dawn of the third day—a fresh start.

My faith encourages me to look for new beginnings at the dawn of each new day. I also noticed it offers more peace of mind than always looking for a bad day. One must "get a life" by moving forward without anticipating a bad event. This reminds me of my old basic-training sergeant who was always screaming out, "Don't anticipate my command!" He knew well that his platoon of soldiers would march very well if they followed his commands. There is no optimism when anticipating only bad events.

Figure 2 symbolizes the results of each new event, new dawns, in my life; and the good events are to be understood.

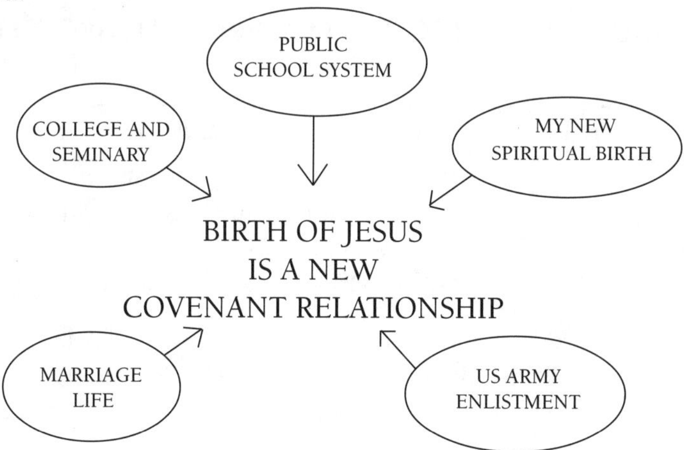

(fig. 2)

Central to everything is my covenant relationship with Jesus. He is like my old sergeant encouraging me not to anticipate a command, which is the work of the Holy Spirit.

The Apostle Paul claimed that one of Jesus' purposes for being with us was "interpreting spiritual things to those who are spiritual" (1 Corinthians 2:13b). I pray daily for a clearer understanding of my Lord's will in my life. The Holy Spirit takes over by arbitrating between Jesus and myself. The Holy Spirit teaches me all I must know (1 Corinthians 2:11).

A professor of mine from Princeton, Dr. James Loder, taught me how each new experience builds upon those that preceded it. He called it the rotation process for growth, illustrating latency patterns. Layering these experiences reveals hidden qualities of one's personality or intelligence. Figure 3 is an example of the rotation process.

ROTATION PROCESS FOR PERSONAL GROWTH

1. Public Schools: GRADUATION	2. Army Life: RESPONSIBILITY, COMMITMENT, SELF-RESPECT
4. College / Seminary: THE LANGUAGE TO COMMUNICATE	3. Marriage: PERSONAL FAMILY DEVELOPEMENT

(fig. 3)

The Holy Spirit was guiding me through all four of those levels. As He did, I began to realize something important about myself. In the first level, I learned about my ability to graduate from high school. During the second level, I learned about responsibility, commitment and self-respect from the US Army. Third, I learned about personal family development from my marriage. And fourth, I learned about communicating. These not only required the ministry of the Holy Spirit, but my hidden, innate, undeveloped abilities had to erupt like a volcano as well. It was liberating. His ministry will continue until our Lord comes again to consummate the kingdom of God.

Perhaps my discussion about the Godhead via these symbols has shown how God operates in our lives. Before I write much more about it, I want to share where and when this concept developed.

The language being used for describing the Godhead / Trinity is similar to the Chalcedon decision of AD 451.[1] It is an image being shared by many Christian denominations. My explanation goes beyond this by showing how God still remains in three illustrations, but the key personality shifts between three ages.

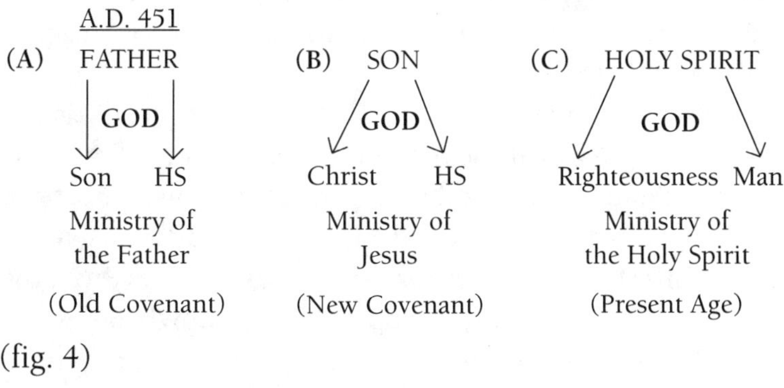

(fig. 4)

Figure 4 illustrates why the Holy Spirit is important in my life. Again, please note how the key personality (top of the diamond shape) changes: (A) has Father, (B) has Son, and (C) has the Holy Spirit. Each key personality became the subject for a particular age. The Heavenly Father revealed Himself as an image of the Almighty (Genesis 17:1) and totally divine (Numbers 23:23; Ezekiel 12:21-28). The Son of God as Jesus also has an active divine role (2 Peter 1:3–4), along with His incarnation (Philippians 2:7).

A and B show two distinct personalities, making it possible to understand how Jesus could talk with the Father while hanging on the cross and how the Father could turn His back on His Son (Mark 15:33–34). A drama of the Godhead was in full action at this point, and therefore the Crucifixion becomes more believable. Going on to example

C, we now have the Holy Spirit ministering to us today; and this has been going on since our Lord's ascension (Luke 24:49; Acts 1:5, 8). For Christians, the Holy Spirit as our righteous God is internally active; but for nonbelievers, He is hidden within their innermost parts and waiting to burst out after a conversion (Genesis 2:7; Proverbs 20:20–27; 2 Corinthians 4:16–18). The importance of the Holy Spirit merits a further study; He is primarily our spiritual teacher (John 16:12–15).

Central to my thesis of the Holy Spirit's ministry is the claim that it began at the moment life was ushered into our bodies (Genesis 2:7). God breathed life into man's nostrils; His Spirit remained hidden until He alerted our conscience to sin in our lives or simply to His existence (Proverbs 20:20–27). Subsequently, people then acknowledge or ignore the Holy Spirit's warnings and existence. For those who believe, the Holy Spirit conducts His teaching ministry in their lives (1 Corinthians 2:11–13). Protecting against compromising our God-given freedom of choice, the Heavenly Father still mandated that the Holy Spirit should nurture our inner human spirit. The Holy Spirit mysteriously and independently moves about within us to accomplish this.

The human spirit has an energy level that can shift into high, neutral or low. The common name given to this energy is our ego or the psyche—from the id. A person who has used the Johnson and Taylor Temperament Analysis Profile would identify the three levels as high = 10–8, neutral = 7–4, and low = 3–1. I often share with my clients who have had a few sessions with me that they keep the Holy Spirit completely out of their life when in the high level.

In the low level, a person is too vulnerable and depressed. I try verbally to take people on a spiritual walk with God, believing the guidance of the Holy Spirit is always with us. We are one in the Spirit and nurtured by the righteous Holy Spirit who performs the will of the Heavenly Father. The human spirit is essentially the image of God without the influence of an ego—the carnal personality.

Some people choose Satan's clever deceptions. He is clearly able to influence a person through the high-level ego by doing cruel things to others. One cruel act is telling false stories about another person, which ultimately destroys the integrity of that person. Although God gave us the freedom to be cruel, it is a sad decision. God allows it because our nature can also be influenced to change for the good. Sometimes people need to die in sin before being resurrected into their new beginning, a positive phenomenon of God's image being partially emulated in our own spirits. We call this wisdom, as known in the lives of Abraham, Moses, Isaac, especially Solomon, Joseph, naturally Jesus of Nazareth, Paul, Eusebius, Martin Luther, John Calvin, John Wesley, and this list can continue. God's divine righteousness enhanced the wisdom of these men when He called them to a divine mission. These men had the same potential to choose cruelty, but they chose to accept God's will (Genesis 22:1–14; Exodus 20:1–26; Deuteronomy 32:48–52; 1 King 3:5–14). History tells of such positive phenomenon in those who are not mentioned in the Bible.

Some Christian denominations teach that one cannot fall from God's grace; this tends to create a dilemma. Admitting guilt is confusing for those Christians who firmly believe they have no choices. This is a myth. The Apostle Paul claimed "all have sinned," but by the abounding grace of Jesus Christ for many there is justification (Romans 5:12–21). There is freedom of choice for all Christians, even under the cloud of shame and guilt. Since they came from sin, Christians have the choice to confess their sin or simply remain in guilt.

One might also want to consider other advice: Shame and guilt should be viewed as a sign coming from God who is actually offering a person the opportunity for repentance. God does not expect us to just suffer in an irreversible situation. Christians can fall from God's grace just as easily as they can also be redeemed. We live in an age of God's grace and the Arbitrator—the Holy Spirit (Ephesians 2:5; John 16:8–15). The Holy Spirit's mission coming from the Heavenly Father extends even further than this level.

In the book *Spiritus Creator* by Regin Prenter, there is a discussion on Martin Luther's doctrine of infused grace as it applies to the Holy Spirit's work. Prenter emphasizes the origins of faith and how a person receives it. As Luther described, faith comes from above—(God's agape love)—and descends into the dwelling Spirit of God. I tried to keep close to Prenter's theory on the Holy Spirit as I developed my own theory. Note a comparison: Prenter says faith comes from above—God's agape love—into our lives from God into the dwelling Spirit of God; I claim the divine powers come from God the Father through the Holy Spirit. I can further illustrate with the egg analogy.

The egg illustrates a continuation of life until the end comes. That life, human power, exists cohesively within the center of the Spirit of Life (God's breath of life), divine power. There is a coexistence of life, the human within the divine. Mr. Prenter used Luther's term, *infused*, but I prefer *cohesion* and *synthesis*. Just as a chick has its whole life ahead after it hatches, so do people. Figure 5 details this description.

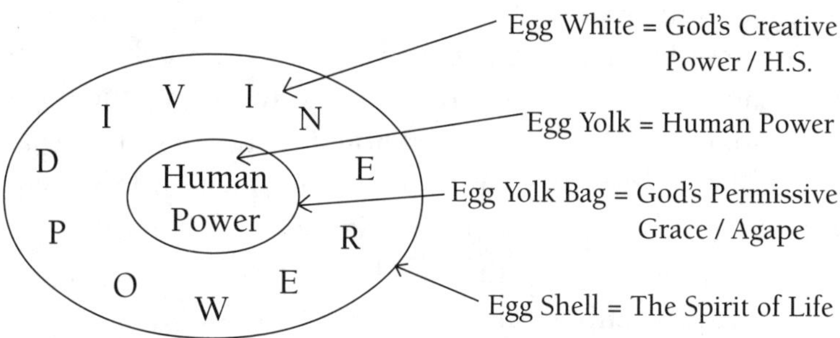

(fig. 5)

The eggshell represents the Spirit of Life that holds one's full potential for sin or spiritual growth. The egg white represents God's creative power being turned over to the Holy Spirit. He raises our consciousness to sin, teaches us about truth, comforts us during troubled times and speaks to the Heavenly Father on our behalf. The yolk bag represents God's permissive grace that shields human power against evil, and yet still allows us to accept evil. We must ask for His protection. The egg yolk itself represents human power that has been given free will to choose between good and evil. Let us now consider these four elements in a more definitive presentation.

The Spirit of Life

God's strategy for a person's full potential within the human power to sin or to gain spiritual growth shall remain the same (Jeremiah 3:12–14; Malachi 3:6; John 1:2; Romans 1:2; and 2 Corinthians 8:19). From the beginning of creation, God created human beings in His own image to have life. There are serious doubts whether God would ever change this plan since He also offers them eternal life. The Heavenly Father ultimately plans to give His people a more complete image, such as what was originally known by Adam and Eve. There is the more conventional theology that Adam and Eve are responsible for the loss of eternal life in the Garden of Eden. One can assume that Jesus will ultimately take us back to the Garden of Eden when He returns to consummate the kingdom of God in the last days. Only the Heavenly Father can cause this to occur.

God's Creative Power: The Holy Spirit

The Heavenly Father turned over His creative powers to the Holy Spirit who raises our consciousness to sin, teaches truth, comforts us during troubled times and speaks to the Heavenly Father on our behalf. He has unlimited divine powers being willed only by the Almighty God. I contend the Holy Spirit not only serves subsequent to the ascension of Jesus, but He also performed numerous tasks for both the Father and the Son of God (Genesis 2:7; Exodus 14:21; Matthew 15:36 & 38, 28:5b–6b; and Acts 3:6, 5:16). Among all these Scriptures, the creative power of the Godhead is identified with the Holy Spirit, but under the authority of the Father or His Son.

I have personally experienced this power. The Holy Spirit did not split any sea for me, but He did multiply bread and communion wafers to more soldiers than was "possible" for the quantity I possessed. My assistant in the reserve unit in Los Angeles got a warm freshly baked loaf of bread, and when he gave it to me I began talking about our Lord's Last Supper. I ate one piece and gave the bread to my assistant. Then he gave it to another soldier after he also took a bite. For an unexplainable and mysterious reason, soldiers in our whole battalion took one bite before the bread was completely gone. Silence took over during the entire experience but was broken by one soldier's quiet question, "Where is the wine?" My assistant and I kept quiet, but we could hardly believe our eyes.

On active duty at Fort Hood, Texas, my assistant always counted the number of communion wafers to make sure they matched the number of soldiers. He also told me that he hoped no one else came to chapel since he could not find any more wafers. However, we got some latecomers from the stockade, and my assistant began to wonder where he could find more wafers. I simply told him not to worry, and even I was amazed after I served the last soldier.

There are many other unexplainable events during my ministry with the soldiers and veterans. The work of the Holy Spirit continues to amaze me, but I accept and believe what He does to glorify the Father.

God's Permissive Grace: Agape Love

God's permissive grace / agape love—the egg yolk bag—shields the human power against evil and yet still allows a person to accept evil. God's nature permits this because of His grace and love for His people. A person's action will always be deliberate and independent from any work or sacrifice he or she makes in life. His permissiveness can be much like a water dam—preventing floods and controlling usage. God could flood us with His overwhelming love, but instead, we have the freedom to control our own intelligent choices. God has no apparent reason to change this practice with His people until the last days.

An overdose of love of any kind, divine or human, has a deadly affect on people. It destroys any potential creativeness in children or adults, single groups or married groups, and in managing any business. God's wisdom has proven to be immensely productive and substantive.

The Human Power

Human power, represented by the egg yolk itself, has been given free will to choose between good and evil. A person is endowed with a limited amount of authority in life, but strong faith empowers a person to accomplish the impossible. In Matthew 17:14–21, Jesus is portrayed as being quite disappointed with His disciples. Their lack of faith in trying to heal the epileptic boy didn't matter to Jesus as much as their lack of faith in the reigning power of God's kingdom. The ultimate process of seeking the kingdom first requires one's faith to be in this kingdom in order to accomplish all things. Healing eventually came from the reigning power of the kingdom and not the disciples' faith in the power of healing.

Jesus considers the reigning power of the kingdom to be of foremost importance for life's journey. It empowers people to accomplish impossibilities, make intelligent decisions and be responsible for all results. Decisions could be anything, such as: building a home, managing a lucrative farm, practicing law or investing in stocks. The reigning power in God's kingdom is a vital part of these decisions, and yet someone still independently makes these decisions.

The conceptualization of the Holy Spirit, God's kingdom and faith should clarify comments from Chapter 1. Perhaps educators and students will consider this as the reason why some people are not able to produce academic excellence. They must be encouraged to take the risk of allowing their suppressed inner human power to burst out for the world to witness and enjoy. No one can predict how long one requires to experience this liberation; I required twenty-two years.

Chapter Three

Educational Synthesis as an Interpretation

Basic to my foundation and power for growth, my conceptualization of the Holy Spirit, God's kingdom and faith have been a learning laboratory. The following study still includes the importance of these three subjects and how they can be supportive to academics. The major emphasis, however, shall operate from the human power.

I want to begin with an interpretation of these three subjects—the Holy Spirit, God's kingdom and faith—in association with God's nature. The term learning laboratory shall be loosely used since learning is not restricted to a classroom lab.

Who can name all the places where occasional learning occurs? Let us compare the practical and academic categories of places where learning can occur.

Practical

- The moment prior to parachuting
- Repelling from a mountain or helicopter
- A rifle assembly room
- Midnight movement field exercise
- Field map reading class
- leadership class: 1st to lead
- First command decision
- First delivery of command briefing

Academic

- Verbalizing learned subjects
- Writing creative theories
- Drawing house blueprints
- First day teaching
- First public speaking
- First debate team
- 1st classroom participation
- Measure knowledge from exams

This comparison between the military and any college course is relevant in content and by being both academic and practical in design. The difference is the outdoor training for the military, but this does not mean there isn't outdoor training for a college class. Some practical courses require students to work on land or farms; to work with people in homes and community projects; or to work with patients in hospitals. These are hands-on training skills that students need. They cannot grasp the full purpose and importance of learning to practice medicine unless they actually take blood from a patient or perform tracheoscopy with a laryngoscope.

I once had an art professor who often used the phrase: "The moment of truth." This became my own quest for knowledge; I also shared it with my students. So, what is this moment of truth? Medical student experience it at the very moment he or she begins to insert the laryngoscope into a patient who jerks from the pain. A colleague of mine, a staff medical doctor, developed an incredible skill in this kind of work. He would tell patients every move he would make while encouraging them to remain still and calm. I never ceased to be inspired by this doctor's abilities. His moment of truth always seemed victorious, but I know he worked hard developing that skill.

When I was in college and three seminaries, teachers were forced to teach between 50 and 100 students in a large classroom. No student could get the quality time with the instructor that might have been required to fully understand the subject. A class of 24 students would be more appropriate. Then the instructor could better assess whether any particular student experienced a moment of truth, grasping the knowledge and skill necessary to fully appreciate a subject. The student who successfully learned ought to be praised for that accomplishment; for those who fail, the instructor and other successful students should tutor them with dignity and respect. This approach will preclude class-insensitive competition that only produces hate, timidity, hurt and high dosages of the ego or id. Classroom environments need to focus on positive results as a model for the future. Let us now examine four positive foundations for a positive learning laboratory.

Positive Freedom for Self-expression

Central to this book has been the suppression of my natural learning ability. I presented a foundation and power that has been hidden in my innermost parts but finally erupted to give me the gift of a liberating life. The importance of the Holy Spirit, God's kingdom and faith became a vital influence on me during this process. It was indeed a positive sense of freedom for my self-expression.

I introduced the moment-of-truth concept and provided a definition of its intended use. Those particular moments are essential since they confirm comprehension; a paratrooper would agree after a successful jump without injury, thereby achieving 100 percent comprehension on the techniques of parachuting. Similar to the previous example of the medical student, the paratrooper endures many hours of positive instruction and practical experience prior to the authorized jump. Any less academic instruction and practicum would surely prove fatal—a costly life of a person. All instructors must remember this fact in order to insist on repetition.

A less dangerous example that contrasts with a paratrooper is a command briefing by a staff officer. A poor presentation is usually interpreted from the extreme embarrassment of the presenting officer, secondary to the officer's interpretation of his or her commander's verbal and facial response. I seldom witnessed this type of embarrassment from staff officers, but it occasionally happened. There is positive training on command briefings, either by the unit command or in the military school system. The primary motivation is a promotion to higher rank. The commander never accepts a poor command briefing. The freedom of self-expression experienced by both the paratrooper and staff officer indeed represents the moment of truth. One might wonder, relative to this moment of truth, how much awareness exists in the majority of people.

Before I met my art professor at the university, I never thought about the moment of truth. In fact, I was only able to associate it with art whenever I painted. I failed to apply it to other courses, such as English, history or the social sciences. I only recall emotional frustration during these courses. Hindsight tells me that other students had a better grasp on the concept. Perhaps some of their discussions, which I found confusing, most likely dealt with their moments of truth. They would make the connection between academic knowledge in history or mathematics and their practical work at the office. Slowly but surely, I finally caught up with the rest by making the same connections.

I decided to take risks in class by offering an opinion during the discussions. I recall the traumatic sound of my loud heartbeat, which no one heard but myself. I began my personal process toward freedom of self-expression by expressing opinions. The more the professors confirmed my answers were correct, the more I edged from a silent mind to a volcanic explosion and liberating life. I brought this gift with me when I taught theology for Saint Leo College. I always tried to support students who seemed to show the same kind of trauma in class discussions. I once conducted an oral exam, which petrified a few students. We had a few moments of small talk until I felt they were calm enough for my questions. They did well.

Nothing can be more damaging than being labeled as stupid. Surely that represents an ultimate unfairness to any person. Unfortunately, a high-school teacher announced before my class peers that there was something she did not like about me, and later the academic advisor told me not to attend college. I also had professors who asked why I was in seminary. There were also classmates who called me stupid. These remarks were totally inappropriate; yet, I chose to continue out my own stubbornness to improve. I eventually learned how God was with me and that He knew my heart, soul and mind.

Chapter 1 dealt with my deficit to learn and communicate ideas. In the 1950s, few specialized remedial study courses were offered in schools. I took a rapid-reading course during the 11th grade, but it did not help me at the time. A remedial English class was offered without credit at most community colleges in 1965, and I found that quite helpful for me. The whole point was to achieve productive study habits—an improvement in reading and writing.

The school system is not the only source for good study habits. The quiet home environment—a room, desk, research books and personal computer—also supports the positive freedom of self-expression. There are retired schoolteachers and business people who would make great mentors for students. A student with that kind of support should do well in college. There are parents without financial means to send their children to college, and there are substandard colleges. Only private enterprise can come to the rescue; the investment would realize a substantial return into the community after these students graduate. Students only need the opportunity to prove it. Thank God for those enterprises that are doing this very thing.

The opportunity for me to return what I learned and to share the possibilities of positive freedom for self-expression occurred during my US Army chaplaincy. I offered soldiers behavioral science classes. There were a few soldiers who could not clearly express themselves. With the help of the Johnson and Taylor Temperament Analysis Profile, I taught them how they could become aware of the strengths and weaknesses of their ego and discussed how they could understand and express their feelings. Later, I privately tutored them in any subject I could. This support eventually encouraged them to take evening college classes on the post. The word must have gotten to the education center at Ft.

Stewart, Georgia, since I was asked to teach theology for Saint Leo College, which has its campus in Saint Leo, Florida. The conclusion here is: The learned person returns the knowledge of positive freedom for self-expression to another learner. Positive learning develops a positive performance

This particular foundation will be quite lengthy since it exists at the heart of a great problem. I also want to remind the reader that some of my recommendations could have easily been resolved subsequent to my teaching tenure during the early 1980s. If *60 Minutes* or *Prime Time Live* offers accurate reports, then my recommendations might possibly be highly relevant for today as well.

There is a sensitive, neutral grade between the reward for an outstanding performance and a degrading evaluation for a poor performance—an average of C. I touched upon this issue in the section, "A Class without Grades." My visit with a mentor of Ph.D. candidates at Oxford taught me that grades A through F cause more emotional disorder than one should allow. How can a positive learning atmosphere develop a positive performance without a grading system? I suggest the use of highly satisfactory or outstanding as ratings and holding the student back until they have achieved it. This will never show a failing grade on a student's transcript. It would not be inappropriate to use the percentage grading system for making a personal judgment of whether or not a student has achieved highly satisfactorily (HS) or outstanding (O): e.g., 80% – 89% = HS and 90%–100% = O respectively. The student who falls below 80 percent is asked to repeat the work until he or she achieves the acceptable level. No student would be given permission to repeat the work after achieving more than 80 percent. This would seem most appropriate for all grades up through high school and undergraduate college. Graduate colleges should accept students who have an outstanding rating in their undergraduate work. And even at the graduate level, both the HS and O should be an acceptable rating to receive a degree. This kind of evaluation would keep the learning laboratory free from high stress and ensure a positive experience.

An academic guidance counselor for a major, such as art or computer science, is essential. I am not aware of any college without this support, but I often hear from other students about being misguided. Students either took a few wrong courses that had nothing to do with their major or they missed a necessary course for graduation. I recall a friend of mine who was held back from graduation until he completed a course. I also was given some wrong advice on required courses; I even had a catalog that gave all the prerequisites. A well-informed guidance counselor will assist a student with a precise guideline, and, in combination with a more effective evaluation of student performance, will further accomplish learning and positive performance.

A relationship between the student and instructor has a great deal to do with a student's performance. I already mentioned about my involvement teaching soldiers and teaching for Saint Leo College. Additionally, I wrote three educational modules to fulfill Dr. Millard R. Shaul's class requirement on liberation theology. The dynamics of learning and performance can be observed.

Let's begin by way of introduction. On a specific morning in a typical city that has a population of 250,000, four young people left on a bus that would take them to a typical US Army training post. Who are they and what was their previous world like? One young man, John, a Caucasian, was known in high school as being a middle-class male chauvinist. Opposing his attitude was Jane, a young Chinese woman that supported the women's liberation movement. George, a black man from the ghetto, was recently given two options in life: to serve a two-year prison term or to serve three years in the US Army. The last person was Lorenzo, a Latino who only completed the ninth grade and barely passed the army's induction tests. These young people represent four distinct worlds and the norm for any unit in today's army.

The following three modules cover how to liberate the oppressed and illustrate a positive relationship between soldiers, who are learning to develop a positive performance, and the chaplain. The setting may not be in the traditional academic environment, but, none the less, college educators can expect the same process. An obvious effort was made to exaggerate the unrest of the unit in order to create a laboratory of learning. Consequently, the modules were not meant for any specific army post. The events are also not representative of my own sessions, but they represent how I generally conduct them.

Module One: A Woman in a Man's Army

This first module will confront the issue of sexism. Through the use of dialogue the goal is to create a sense of liberation for those who are caught in the oppression of sexism and still need to function within a military system. John and Jane represent the total population of an army signal battalion. Their responses will be representative of that group.

Chaplain-1: On this large newsprint, I wrote: "A Woman in a Man's Army." Respond to it any way you like. [The chaplain points to the written statement.]

JOHN-1: Right on man—right on! The army really has flipped out. I mean, I'm getting fed up doing both my work and the work these chicks refuse to do.

JANE-1: OK, you chauvinist pig, what work have you done for me?

JOHN-2: Don't you remember the guard duty I pulled for you and the many times you asked me to lift the heavy radio equipment?

JANE-2: What do you expect from a woman?

JOHN-3: One minute you cry out, "Equal rights!" and the next you ask me to treat you like a woman. I'm confused; what do you mean?

JANE-3: Why can't you understand? I'm merely asking you for the freedom to do what I desire. I have both strengths and weaknesses: strength in the skill of working on radios, and a weakness in standing guard or engaging in combat. I simply want to experience a greater personhood within myself. I enjoy some of the feminine roles, such as expressing emotions, being disorganized, or being soft and weak. I accept these roles for my own reasons and not because a man says that I must. A man has no right to project in me how I must act or what I must do. The only right a man has is to honor the strengths and weaknesses I have.

CHAPLAIN-2: OK…I'm grateful for your enthusiasm. From this dialogue, it appears that John bought into the statement I wrote down, and Jane didn't. [Pause] As I listened to both of you, I heard a clear message from Jane. I'm wondering, John, whether you would tell us what Jane's message was.

JOHN-4: Jane told me that she is a person who has the right to determine her own roles and life. She also accepts her strengths and weaknesses.

CHAPLAIN-3: Precisely, John. Let's try to prepare a list of some stereotypical roles our society has placed on women and men. [The process goes on for about a period of fifteen minutes. The list consists of the content below.]

Stereotypes For

Men	**Women**
1. Bread winner	1. Domestic work
2. Boss	2. Motherhood
3. Stoic	3. Emotional
4. Rational / Thinker	4. Intuitive / Feelings
5. Organized	5. Disorganized
6. Concrete	6. Idealistic
7. Rugged	7. finesse
8. Men driver	8. Women driver
9. Aggressive	9. Submissive / Sex object
10. Loud spoken	10. Soft / Weak
11. Athletic	11. Artistic
12. Forthright	12. Manipulative

CHAPLAIN-4: I think we have a partial list that will fulfill our objective. [A pause occurs as everyone reviews the list.] Jane, would you please tell us what this list says to you?

JANE-4: It says the male's list is best.

CHAPLAIN-5: How is the male's list best?

JANE-5: The man's world dictates both lists, and, not only that, the man made himself out as an almighty hero. If you study that list, you may agree that men would quickly accept that list as being valid. Why? The reason is simply centered around the common fact that a man placed these roles on a woman.

CHAPLAIN-6: John, what do you think of Jane's comment?

JOHN-5: I agree with the female's list, and I guess Jane is right.

JANE-6: I know I'm right. Both lists are excellent examples of sexism, and that always says that a man is better than a woman.

CHAPLAIN-7: Thank you....Now, we learned that these roles were written by men and that they have the best list. Such roles lead to an identity crisis for women and, hence, the next point: the identity crisis of women [Chaplain points again to the next section on the newsprint.]:

Identity Crisis for Women

AGE 13	AGE 20	AGE 40
Must become lady-like	Decision to make as to whom she is" educator, nurse, wife, ????.	Who/What am I? What is my purpose for living? What about after the children leave?

CHAPLAIN-8: Now that we have looked at this statement on the identity crisis of women, what is your reaction or comments?

JANE-7: I feel that sense of double-bind again. [Pause]

CHAPLAIN-9: Would you care to pursue that feeling further?

JANE-8: As I said earlier, I enjoy some of the female roles we saw on the list, but I also enjoy doing a role that may not be a female role. My job is a good example of that....

This dialogue continues until the chaplain completes the goal: to create, among all the young people, a sense of liberation from the oppression of sexism that will still function within a military system. In essence, the concept of the modern volunteer army would support a goal of this nature. All commanders have the responsibility to operate under such a concept and still accomplish the mission.

Herein lies the axiom from which all decisions are made: a commander must achieve the mission given from a higher command. The mission is the first objective for any command, and all else comes afterwards. For the purpose of this module, the commander decided to resolve the unrest within the unit over sexism with the assistance of the chaplain. Solving this unrest ultimately would have a positive affect upon the mission of the unit.

As a conclusion to Jane's comment in Jane-8, we can affirm her decision in life. In addition to affirming, the chaplain provided further guidance in order to help the group members make their own decisions.

Within the military system, all personnel must become aware of the commander's mission, which was presented. Each person must expect a loss of some freedom normally available in civilian life. One adjusts only by coping with the loss of that freedom. A very realistic philosophy is that each person does an equal share of work. Jane needs to become more aware of the commander's responsibility and accept her share of an equal work load. Pulling guard in the command headquarter area, for example, would be considered a fair expectation of a commander. John, on the other hand, needs to become aware of how he and Jane, together, can mature into stronger personalities. Losing the popular male's aggressive control over females will become a gain for John's life. After John and Jane become aware of these things and make the decision to accept them, the condition of sexism will be resolved until another group of young people enters the unit. Within the context of this class, positive learning certainly developed a positive performance among the young people in the battalion.

Module Two: Liberation from Racism

The second module is designed to confront military people with the issue of racism. The case of George is representative of many Blacks, but he demonstrates how he takes charge of his own anger through the process of positive learning. The class session begins.

CHAPLAIN-1: Statistics tell me that our post consist of 22 percent Black, 2 percent Asian, 6 percent Latinos, and 70 percent Whites. Lately, all of us have learned about a fatal tragedy that was a direct result of racial disharmony. Obviously something is happening. These statistics and this incident relate to each other only in the sense that it is time to take a good look inward. Our purpose for the next two hours is to do just that.

Let's begin with some speculation. Suppose we say that some people are suffering from injustice and exploitation under this command. [The chaplain writes down "injustice" and "exploitation" on the newsprint pad, and everyone looks for a moment at the two words.] Who cares to respond to these words?

GEORGE-1: I know the word injustice, but what does exploi...ta...tion mean?

CHAPLAIN-2: I'm sure you've heard the expression, "I've been had."

GEORGE-2: Ohhh, *did* I! Ha, ha....That's been my life. Ever since I can remember, I lived with rats that nearly ate me up once and still the rent was too damn high. In school, when something went wrong, somehow I had to be guilty. The last time that happened, the "man" gave me a choice: spend two years in the pen or three years here in the army. When something goes wrong here, Top [First Sergeant] comes to me. Injustice, exploi…tation… Hell, don't tell me what they mean—I *know*!

CHAPLAIN-3: You sound hurt and angry.

GEORGE-3: Damn right I'm hurt and angry. I'm always wrong. Top gets on my case when I'm five minutes late to formation or when he thinks I lipped off. I never do things right.

CHAPLAIN-4: I understand your hurt and anger. Obviously I cannot say that I have experienced what you have; it would be ridiculous for me to say so. But let's look at the issues you raised, George. We first can write down key words that would identify your issues. [Chaplain writes down the following issues: "(1) Exploited by landowners, (2) Blacks studying in Whites' educational system and (3) civilian culture in a military culture."] George, would you study these issues for a moment and respond any way you feel toward them?

GEORGE-4: (Pause] Damn it! I feel put down.…I'm not an equal, let alone better than someone.

CHAPLAIN-5: What can you do?

GEORGE-5: Nothing. The white man has the power now.

CHAPLAIN-6: Today, the white man has the power; but tomorrow, if the black man takes power, then what can you do?

GEORGE-6: I can annihilate the white man. Nothing else can be done. As long as the white man lives, Blacks will always be the underdog.

CHAPLAIN-7: Your hope for equality is seen after there is total annihilation of the white man. Did I understand you right?

GEORGE-7: You're right. Blacks and Whites have talked long enough. The white man has no intention to change.

CHAPLAIN-8: George, as I said before...my world is different from yours, but I want to struggle with you as we look deeper at those issues. Can you trust me as we do this together?

GEORGE-8: OK, I can trust you a little. What do you have in mind?

CHAPLAIN-9: I want to begin with what I sense you have said to me. Did you say in so many words that you feel boxed in or, to use a popular expression: oppressed?

GEORGE-9: Let me think...yes.

CHAPLAIN-10: Then, as means to counteract that, you decided to annihilate the oppressor—the white man—as the best solution. Is that correct?

GEORGE-10: You're right.

CHAPLAIN-11: OK...In the course of time, many Blacks now are saying two things: First, violence is no longer necessary since changes are taking place. Second, a growing awareness of racial identity—roots—is being established in other races, too, since the Black liberation movement begun. Many races are coming together now to unite in a loving spirit. In fact, Malcolm X expressed how impressed he was at this during his personal pilgrimage to Mecca prior to his unfortunate death. I'm sure you know well the feelings he had toward the white man. The Muslim leaders as well as many black Christian leaders are preaching this spirit of love. The list is very long, but the late Dr. Martin Luther King, Jr. and Tom Skinner are two outstanding Christian men who preached this idea. George, what do you want to say at this point?

GEORGE-11: I don't remember some of the things you said, but I'm glad they happened. I didn't know so many brothers said those things, and I can't understand why. Do you suppose, chaplain, it might be where I lived and the way I lived that caused my hate?

CHAPLAIN-12: What do you think?

GEORGE-12: I'm sure you're right.

CHAPLAIN-13: You seem to be looking at yourself more. Were you blaming the White man completely, or do you think everyone is a sinner, and now all must ask forgiveness together?

GEORGE-13: I was looking only at the White man. It's good to know that other brothers see a change, and some of the Whites are helping. I hope changes can happen in me.

CHAPLAIN-14: I am happy with you, George, for your new awareness. You were on the right track when you began with yourself. Let's look at a couple of things you mentioned earlier. You mentioned the time when you came five minutes late to formation, and your problem with authority when the first sergeant got after you. Would you agree with this?

GEORGE-14: You're right. I don't understand what to do.

CHAPLAIN-15: Perhaps I can help all of us understand by creating a situation to solve. Let's start where we are. We are in the army, and we know that the system within the army only operates under one basic plan—army regulations. We learned that commanders have one primary job—to do the mission. Now, does it matter under these regulations whether the commander is a man, woman, Black or White?

GEORGE-15: No. I see what you are saying. A pink woman would do the same thing to me as Top.

CHAPLAIN-16: Precisely! We are fighting a regulation most of the time. Let's not fool ourselves, either. We already know that people do the wrong things.

The first sergeant can be wrong, but that is another issue. Let's just stay with your statement: A "pink" woman would do the same things. Why? She only does what she is told.

GEORGE-16: I see. I suppose formation times fall under the same regulations.

CHAPLAIN-17: No regulation says that a first sergeant will call a formation at such-and-such time, but it does say that the first sergeant will inform the troops and take a head count of all personnel. The formation is important for that purpose as well as the job that is done after the formation is held. The longer one person holds up the total group, the less amount of work everyone will accomplish. Additionally, the head count is the best way to maintain the availability of all troops. One missing person could signal something is seriously wrong with that person.

GEORGE-17: I was being very selfish. I never thought Top felt any of us were that important. He wants me to be part of the team, and safe as well. I like that, and I'm going to help out by getting to the formations on time.

CHAPLAIN-18: Frankly, George, I never thought about it in those terms. You are absolutely right. I learned something just then, too. Thank you.

GEORGE-18: What am I going to say? Ha, ha [both laugh].

Anyone's guesses as to whether that dialogue was realistic or not is as good as mine. I am inclined to say that its realism is too close to refute. It closely follows with Gutierrez's viewpoint of faith:[2] A Christian's faith is expressed through a genuine commitment to liberate the oppressed. By being as realistic as possible, I attempted to express the commitment I have to the oppressed and how I learned to remain open in a fluid, two-way dialogue. The technique serves well for positive learning.

Within the dialogue, I asked three important questions: (1) What is the meaning of George's struggle? (2) What are his options and what do they mean? (3) What was significant in George's history and what should it mean for his future? Obviously my goal was to create a new understanding within the man and, ironically, for myself as well. I became aware of something new in the military. This kind of new awareness in our own life often occurs between a teacher and student. One of my professors told us that we could teach him something new. I could not understand how, since he was a holder of three doctorate degrees, an authority on the Old and New Testaments, and he knew twenty languages.

This second module certainly demonstrated positive learning and how to increase positive performance.

ModuleThree: Pedagogy of the Oppressed

This module represents my own experience as a student in high school, but let us keep in mind that Lorenzo, who represents many struggling soldiers with little education, was given a class concerning a pedagogy of the oppressed; I wasn't.

Setting: The staff chaplain recently advised the post commander of a notable trend among the recently enlisted military people, and further recommended conducting a class on the pedagogy of the oppressed. His justification was based on the fact that there had apparently been pressure on the US Army recruiting program to maintain quotas, which required lowering the army's educational standards (a minimum for enlistment was a high-school diploma or GED). Recent studies given to the chaplains bore out the shocking fact that 36 percent of those recruited only completed the ninth grade and barely passed the army's induction tests. This told young recruits that they were educationally qualified. However, later, these same recruits were informed that they did not have the required level of education at their permanent duty station.

The unfairness of this situation was soon recognized. This not only had a negative affect on these soldiers, but the commander's mission suffered immensely as well. The commander then issued an order to all the subordinate commanders requiring a resolution to this situation through the professional guidance of their unit chaplains. Perhaps the following would occur.

CHAPLAIN-1: The unit commander has expressed a sincere concern about the fact that too many personnel do not have a high-school education. Putting aside the army's basic requirement to insure a minimum of a high-school education before enlistment for all personnel, the commander and I prefer to identify with you and your struggles to achieve that goal. The commander has established appropriate hours and priorities to achieve this task. We have organized a program with the education officer for those who will be attending. Upon completion of the course, each will receive a diploma from the high school in his or her hometown or from our local school board. After saying this, would anyone care to share the kind of educational experience you've had?

LORENZO-1: I do. I completed the ninth grade, and I'm not sure what I learned; I don't even understand why.

CHAPLAIN-2: Do you recall what you felt during those class periods?

LORENZO-2: Stupid and unknown. I remember a few students who always talked with the teacher and one or two others could never get the teacher's attention. They sometimes would raise their hands for a whole hour and still fail to be recognized.

CHAPLAIN-3: I noticed you didn't include yourself with the others.

LORENZO-3: I couldn't say anything. I'm really surprised that I'm talking now. Somehow you make me feel relaxed.

CHAPLAIN-4: You look confident in yourself.

LORENZO-4: Oh, man...that's a change.

CHAPLAIN-5: Your willingness to talk makes you look that way.

LORENZO-5: You mean, when I didn't talk, then I looked like I was unwilling to talk? That's the reason the teacher never called on me!

CHAPLAIN-6: Sometimes it might work out that way. Remember the other students who were never called upon?

LORENZO-6: Oh, yeah.

CHAPLAIN-7: Teachers have the same responsibility as the students: They should talk and recognize others just like during any conversation. Education is an experience when everyone learns.

LORENZO-7: You mean, the teacher learns too?

CHAPLAIN-8: Usually....I learn something during classes like this. No one stops learning, and everyone has something to teach. Education is so wonderful when you realize that you are a major part of that process.

LORENZO-8: How can I become a major part?

CHAPLAIN-9: Each person is vital to the other and possesses an equal potential of learning. When the silent person doesn't contribute to the class discussion, they don't learn, and they could be the crucial link to the best results from the class as a whole. For this reason a person is always a major part of the group. I always share a somewhat snappy phrase: The learned person returns the knowledge of positive freedom for self-expression to a learner.

LORENZO-9: Wow! I never thought of that. I can see now why I felt unknown. If I am on the receiving end as the learner, then I, too, will find knowledge to pass on as well. I think this explains a little as to why I felt stupid. What am I missing? I still think there is something else.

CHAPLAIN-10: Perhaps you felt you had nothing valuable to offer.

The dialogue continues, and hopefully Lorenzo has begun a new and exciting life of learning and sharing positive knowledge about self-expression. The class objective was to create a new self-awareness among the personnel. For our purpose, Lorenzo achieved it. The chaplain continued in this dialogue with Lorenzo and others that had questions. A member of the education center was with this class toward the end of the period to instruct how one registers for classes and, later, earn a high-school diploma. Others who have the diploma already were excused from the classroom.

The purpose for conducting a class on the pedagogy of the oppressed in a military unit is to emphasize that the command can become a positive encouragement to the staff members of the education center. The command can help if two things are in order.

1. The commander has a sincere concern for the welfare of his or her personnel.
2. Teachers follow good, pupil-centered concepts of teaching, such as Paulo Freire's.

Surely all army personnel, as well as all students, have the right to receive an opportunity for the best education possible. For educators, this module focuses on the positive learning process that leads to positive performance. Whereas the focus was on proceeding from learning to performance, note also that oppression was another issue involved besides sexism, racism and pedagogy. This issue falls on the teacher's responsibility to communicate to the students and remain committed. Now having the experience of being both a student and teacher, I fully appreciate the importance of communicating the course textbook and all other related materials.

Typically, Sunday school teachers in small churches have a history of teaching without the full knowledge of the Bible, how to use it or how to communicate its content. Much of the problem is not a lack of concern or respect but simply a lack of training. A small congregation cannot immediately afford to begin an adequate program, but their desire for it minimizes their willingness to invest in well-organized teacher training. Their Bible training and pupil relationship should include four important prerequisites:

1. **A Teacher's Knowledge of the Bible:** An important prerequisite for a healthy class is that the teacher must possess a functional knowledge of the Bible. Therefore, periodically, a director of religious education in churches should offer teacher training so new teachers can learn how to study the Bible, how to study commentaries and how to teach a

Bible class. The young men and women or children are not looking for trite, stereotypical theology but substantive answers to contemporary questions. Christ is the supreme example of how one should answer contemporary questions. The main emphasis, then, is to focus on people. A newcomer to any group seldom feels welcome just as he or she is—a person with needs and potentials.

2. **The Matter of Being Interested:** A young adult usually has at least one hobby he or she enjoys, be it hunting, baseball, tennis, sewing or whatever. He or she will tend to know everything there is to know about the hobby merely because of the interest they have in it. As a contrast, most young boys do not care about English grammar. There is no interest, and, hence, they do not learn. What does this say to the teacher? An interest must be aroused before learning takes place. But how is interest generated? At this point, a teacher utilizes his / her understanding of students via their needs. Students usually gain respect for their teacher and the Bible after their needs are met.

There are a number of people in positions of authority supporting the above recommendations: Dr. Findley B. Edge, professor at Southern Baptist Theological Seminary; Robert S. Clemmons, an author; and Dr. Emil Brunner, a theologian. Dr. Edge's view on learning suggests a consideration of, "[An individual as a person has] experience and…knowledge…[with] value. The pupil is a responsible member of the learning group, both having something to contribute and having something to learn. The needs and interests of the pupil serve as a guide for the teacher in knowing what to teach and how to teach."[3] Both the student and teacher should be actively engaged in seeking to discover the truth that meets needs. This process places the responsibility upon the students to discover that truth. And as Dr. Edge suggested, a person will immediately become interested when he or she realizes someone cares about his or her needs. He therefore concludes that interest is inherent in the learning activity itself.

3. **Relationship between People:** Robert S. Clemmons, in his two books, Dynamics of Christian Adult Education and Education for Churchmanship, contends that the leader and the learner must understand what is happening during their learning experience. Love and understanding must be expressed in the group, and the Spirit of Christ must be allowed to work within the group. Each person involved should recognize and treat the others as a people. The group should develop a person-to-person learning experience. For example, during the fellowship between person A and person B, person A can learn that person B has certain human characteristics which make him or her unique and beautiful. Person A, therefore, accepts person B for who he or she is—and vice versa.

An adult group can become an example of spiritual power by sharing religious experiences; people will gain insight and learn new meanings. As they relate with each other, change will occur. They will learn their abilities and shortcomings. They will become aware of their ultimate dependence upon God. Christian fellowship, then, is essential for one to grow spiritually.

Dr. Emil Brunner says: "And likewise in faith I do not think, but God leads me to think; He does not communicate 'something' to me, but 'Himself.' The counterpart is no longer as in thinking a something, a something pondered and discussed which I infer through the energy of my thinking, but a person who Himself speaks and discloses Himself, who Himself thus has the initiative and guidance and takes over the role…which in thinking I have myself. An exchange hence takes place here which is wholly without analogy in the sphere of thinking. The sole analogy is in the encounter between human beings, the meeting of person with person."[4] It appears Brunner views a relationship between people as being like a person's relationship with God, relative to the faith that person has. God leads one to think, just as teachers can do for their students. God does not communicate something but Himself, just as the teacher can do as well. There is no analysis but what occurred between the teacher and student who made a contact with each other.

Finally, the student alone has the initiative and guidance to take over the role of a teacher. Each student can be assigned a particular theme or an issue in a textbook to teach the whole class. This same assignment will also work well for small groups. Each group can discuss a topic, decide together all the important facts and then present their results to the class. Mr. Clemmons summarized for leaders and class members that all should:

a) "Create a climate of Christian fellowship in their group."
b) "Listen with understanding to the contributions of others."
c) "Assist the group in clarifying alternatives, making decisions, and proposing plans."
d) "Delegate authority to others and trust in their creative ability to get things done."
e) "Be aware of personal needs of others and seek to respond in a Christian way."

f) "Keep growing as they gain insights, test experiences, use their best spiritual and ethical judgments, and change as they work out a better way of living together."

He went on to note that a learning experience requires sensitivity to the readiness of adults, flexibility in approach and understanding of the way adults learn.[5] When does learning take place? Learning occurs when the teacher is concerned for the needs of a person; when a dynamic method is employed; when good, honest communication occurs through an interpersonal relationship; when students respond to the teacher's creativity, spontaneity and appreciation; and when the gospel is integrated as a personal word from God.

4. **Exposure to new ideas:** How are new ideas introduced into a class? Harold D. Minor presented six ways.[6]

1) "Present new ideas unselfconsciously and with confidence."
2) "Relate the presentation of new ideas with care."
3) "Relate new ideas to the total discussion."
4) "Teach so that new ideas enter the class from many sources."
5) "Be aware of how the congeniality of the group affects its readiness to face new ideas. The learner will not care about the teacher's new ideas unless the teacher first cares about the learner."
6) "Finally, clarify each new idea by contrasting it with opposing ideas."

Ideas are also introduced through various kinds of teaching methods. Mr. Wayne R. Rood suggested useful diagrams.[7] The T represents *teaching*, C is *content*, and the L is *learner*.

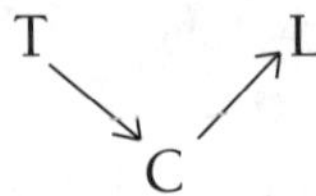

The teacher is active. Content will be as good as the teacher.

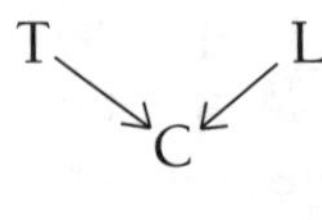

The content is passive here. Data and facts are usually included in the content. Note that both T and L are active now and meet at C.

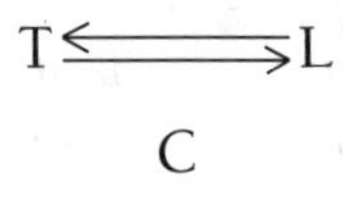

Through discussions, T and L meet directly without regard of C. The purpose is to learn self.

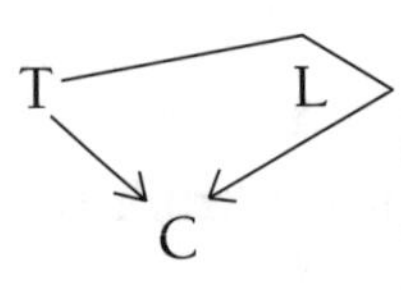

Martin Buber's concept: T is actively concerned about both L and C. Note that T can "see" or experience C from L's point of view. L joins T and C, and both T and L became learners in relation to C. This concept is based upon a warm and creative Judaic philosophy.

When C is the Christian gospel, a new dimension is thrust into the situation: ground of communication (GC).

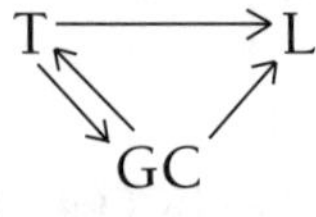

All are active here. C means a ground of communication. T and GC draw responses from L.

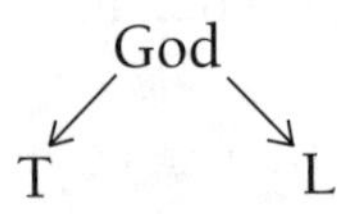

The encounter method begins with God addressing both T and L. Each will reply.

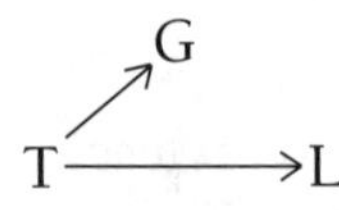

T replied which became the ground for discussion.

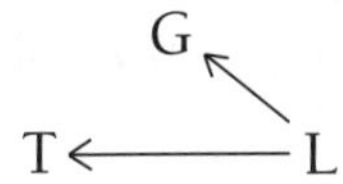

This discussion became the ground for L to respond.

Much of the presentation, thus far, under Bible knowledge and pupil relationship, has been borrowed from very reliable sources. In them, the main emphasis is to focus on the people, their needs and their potential to learn. The teacher has the responsibility to meet these needs and introduce new ideas so truth can be discovered. Thus, the goal of establishing a relationship is fulfilled. However, the four educational techniques that are about to be introduced should provide a deeper understanding of how new ideas can be exposed to students.

1. The Colloquy Method:

This consists of a panel discussion between a resource person from the group, a moderator and the colloquy—the balance of the group. The moderator has the responsibility to explain in detail to the resource person what colloquy means and its purpose. Further, the moderator is to study the characteristics of students and then be flexible and informal. The purpose of the colloquy is to accomplish eight steps:[8]

1. Stimulate interest in a topic.
2. Identify, clarify, or solve problems.
3. Identify or explore issues.
4. Bring expert knowledge to bear on problems and needs as they emerge from discussions.
5. Give the audience opportunity to understand the component parts of a topic.

6. Weigh the advantages and disadvantages of a course of action.
7. Reduce the natural barriers that usually stand between a large audience and resource person, thereby helping to establish rapport between the audience and those on the platform.
8. Offer resource persons the opportunity to get a clear picture of the audience's knowledge of the topic(s).

The importance for an evaluation by students and the teacher cannot be overly emphasized. The process can be accomplished by written or oral questions. One can use the following questions, but others may surface during the colloquy experience.

- What was learned from this experience?
- What was known previously?
- Was the time well spent or wasted?
- What did the resource person learn from the colloquy members?
- What did the moderator learn?
- What are possible suggestions for improvement?

2. The Field-Trip Method:

The field trip should be an educational tour in which a group of students visits a place of interest for firsthand observation and study. The instructor must explain to the group that a guide will be with them to explain features most people seldom recognize but which have some significance to observe. The group should also be encouraged to ask questions about anything they do not understand. After the field trip a careful analysis, interpretation or discussion of the trip should be given. The Colloquy Method could be used at this time or just an informal discussion where every member of the group has equal opportunity to respond. One person, however, should be appointed to take notes so a time of recapitulation can follow the discussion. An evaluation of this discussion should be made privately by the instructor. When should the field trip be used?

1, It should be used to provide firsthand observation and study of something that cannot be brought to the students.
2. It should stimulate interest and concern about conditions or problems that need study.
3. It should illustrate the result of practice or a course of action in its natural environment.
4. It should relate theoretical study to practical application.[9]

With a little bit of collective luck, these efforts should produce positive learning and performance in all the students. A good example of a firsthand trip could be to the Holy Land; one can gain a sense of where Jesus had His ministry or how many faiths of today assemble for their own pilgrimages.

3. The Quiet-Meeting Method:

This is an attempt to let the Spirit of Christ take over for the purpose of teaching—teachers from secular schools could label this time: "Quiet Time for Reflection"—and it tends to be a practice seldom used. The purpose is to integrate all previously learned materials. One should allow fifteen to sixty minutes for these sessions.

The technique consists of quietness and occasional spontaneous verbal contributions by any member of the group. The silence includes meditation (concentration) and study on the topic that has been placed before them on the chalkboard or easel. Freedom of expression is strongly emphasized; one contribution should not necessarily be built upon the other. This is an effective way to summarize several methods of study. A private evaluation by the instructor should be made following the meeting.

WARNING: All members of the group must know each other well. Before each session, about ten minutes should be given to get acquainted with any new person and to ask how each have been since the last meeting. This meeting should be held when everyone feels the need for it. Above all, the instructor should be sensitive to group feelings. If one person occasionally monopolizes the session, then a private talk afterwards will usually solve the problem.

4. The Role-Playing Method

The purpose is to emphasize relationships among people. Role-playing must portray typical attitudes rather than special acting abilities. Group members are chosen to assume roles and act out a real-life, problem situation. For example: An instructor may want to ask one student to imagine being a well-known person who has been encountered by another well-known person, played by student number two. While acting out these roles, they may totally forget the context in which they presently live and attempt to be the person they portray.

A discussion should follow the role-play. The class tries to learn how the actors felt during the play and compare feelings with others in the class. Several trials can be made to determine alternative forms of behavior. Caution should be used to make sure no one leaves with hurt feelings or that they're confused.

Holy Spirit. He comes when infants are tortured to death, when women are sexually assaulted, when massive numbers of people are killed (like the Oklahoma City bombing) and when any other human disaster occurs. The Holy Spirit reaches out and grasps the hands of those unfortunate victims who have called out for help and offers the glory of God's lovingkindness. His power manifests in this new birth; He restores their soul for an eternal relationship and for stronger faith to face the future. For those who remain alive after a traumatic disaster, those people cease to be the same individuals they were in the old life. They become a new creature in Christ, similar to our day of salvation.[10]

God's Power Restructures Lives

Most versions of the Bible use the word renewal; I tend to favor restructure to denote the concept of restoration of spiritual strength subsequent to a new birth. The event should never be considered as a one-time occasion. The number of occasions when God needs to restructure our lives varies. Scripture supports the notion that God is willing to restore us, especially the mind.[11] The Holy Spirit wants to restructure the frustrated mind by offering peace. I cannot think of anything worse than having to suffer from a schizophrenic mind. I firmly believe the Holy Spirit played a vital part in restructuring my mind to function more clearly and more creatively. There are vast differences between confused people with severe psychological disorders and my learning deficit—a hidden potential for learning.

God only requires a pure heart. He simply expects us to worship Him as God Almighty, acknowledge Christ as Lord, and respond to an awareness of our sins—the Holy Spirit in our conscience—by confessing and repenting of these sins. God cares about the life we have, and, occasionally, He reveals a specific plan for us to fulfill. We can reject it or be committed to it. When God chooses to break through my life with a plan, I try to understand it and become committed to it. Jesus' example for us to imitate consists of the following:[12]

1. Jesus looked for men who were willing to be committed to Him and to follow Him.
2. He built a group of men who were committed to each other.
3. He developed within the group a consciousness of being committed to the kingdom's work for the rest of their lives.
4. The group's security was centered in the person of Christ and not in a program.
5. Jesus ministered to people where they were. He developed a web of relationships within the group that resulted in greater awareness of each individual's needs.

The Holy Spirit continues to support the effects of Jesus by teaching us how to accomplish them. A teacher would do well to learn them and decide how to use them in class. Together, the teacher and the Holy Spirit can have a positive impact on the student.

The Positive Importance of Celebrating Achievement

The moment of truth always seems very special and is something one tends never to forget. It is an event that surely deserves great celebration. The paratrooper can be ever so joyful after he or she successfully jumps. I can hear that person shout, "Yes, yes, yes!" with a clinched fist and a wide grin on the face. It would indeed be an important and positive celebration of that achievement. Relatives and friends would most likely join that celebration. Graduates from West Point would toss their caps, a new father would pass out cigars and candy after the birth of a child, the newly selected Miss America sheds tears of immense joy, and the Olympic gold-medallist quivers and sheds tears of extreme joy while standing before his / her nation's flag and mumbling the national anthem. They, too, have the right to an important positive celebration over their achievements. Who would be silly enough to deny them?

Students in any class have the same right to a celebration of achievement. It motivates them to excel further. Celebrations are much more positive than the "rat race" of achieving Bs and As. I have already dealt with the tragedy that results from using the A-through-F grading system. It carries over to the business world and money becomes the focus more than the welfare of people. Our society ends up with only cold-heartedness, which belies the fabric of human nature. There is a definite correlation between this grading system and greed. Motivation is a driving force, and I'd rather see it used in a positive sense.

The celebration of achievement motivates students to further their studies. A break between the AA and the BA degrees, or the BA and MA degrees, is a positive recommendation for students. They can either work for a business without having to worry about a high salary, or they can take a trip to a foreign country—if they have the money. These are ways to celebrate, a time for reflection on their achievement and a time to evaluate their final vocation. After studying, the mind deserves a rest of 1 to 2 years, or one will miss a great opportunity for another level of educational maturity. My practical experience in the US Army should serve as a background and justification for taking a break. My achievement was a liberating life from silence.

CONCLUSION

The Kingdom of God

The central theme in the message and ministry of Jesus was the kingdom of God. In the Bible, the word God was occasionally replaced with heaven. Both words have a specific meaning. Both Jesus and John the Baptist, a cousin of Jesus, began their ministry with the message: "Repent ye; for the kingdom of heaven is at hand" (Matthew 3:2; 4:17). Jesus defined His mission as "I must preach the good tidings of the kingdom of God to other cities also: for there too was I sent" (Luke 4:43). Although our first example used the word heaven for describing the kingdom, the second example used the word God. Both mean that the kingdom, indeed, belongs only to God. Any other reason for a difference between using God and heaven is in reverence to the Almighty Heavenly Father.

Why should the word God be used for the statement: "The kingdom of God actively works in our lives"? My reference is either to Christ or the Holy Spirit, since both are in the Godhead. The kingdom of God ministers to people who are filled with confusion, hate, distrust, etc., by removing these negative qualities and filling them with love, an overwhelming trust of Christ, a clear mind and many other blessings. A whole new outlook in life is created for that person. Although Christ and the Holy Spirit perform this mission, the Almighty Heavenly Father wills it to happen. We, therefore, can say that the kingdom of heaven is "at hand" for those people.

Christian Faith

The very moment Christians receive their faith from God, an enriched refinement of their faith begins (Luke 8:22–25). So it was during the transition between Jesus' ministry of three years and the apostolic ministry in the church. Faith may mean faithfulness (trustworthiness) in God's grace for Israel's history, but it now lays hold of the saving act in Christ, the origins of salvation (Acts 4:12). A Christian's obedience in faith no longer trusts in the Ten Commandments but rather in the way of salvation.[13] There is confidence in Christ as well as His Father. If we are dead in Christ, we shall also live with Him eternally.[14]

Faith expresses the beginning and end of human life. Jesus' life had a physical beginning and ending. Mortal human beings also share in these same physical experiences. Where do we differ from Jesus? We certainly differ by not being an immortal God. The mortal flesh of Jesus on earth obviously died on the cross, but the immortal God in Jesus never died and lives eternally. We cannot be any more different than this. We therefore need no other reason for believing, trusting, reaching out to and holding on to this gospel message of salvation.

Our Use of Divine Love

The word love in the English language has its limitation. It is used in the sense of a strong affection for, attachment for or a devotion to someone; a strong liking for or interest in something; a strong, usually passionate, affection for a person of the opposite sex.*

In theology, the word is used in the sense of God's benevolent concern for His people; His people's devout attachment to God. Love, under the Hebrew or Greek context, can be summed up by an earnest and anxious desire for, and an active and beneficent interest in, the well-being of the word love. The use of love is twofold: (1) We have a vertical love relationship between God and His people, and (2) we have the horizontal love relationship between ourselves and other people. God's love is indeed active with both relationships. Whereas we can experience God's direct love between Him and us on the vertical level, we shall also experience the results of God's love on the horizontal level. These love-sharing experiences are relative to God's image; it's one more example of God's people being like Him, in His own image (Genesis 1:26).

These three spiritual factors were central to my educational maturity, and it is my hope that they were presented fairly and truthfully. It is finally my hope that this book becomes a foundation to other books that will show many more examples of how God works in our lives.

Addendum One

Wake Up to the Bible

Wake up to the Bible! When will we ever understand a very important message from the Old Testament prophets? The Minor Prophets had a message: "Our prophecies are relevant." I contend that if the Minor Prophets are relevant, then, their message along with the total content of the Bible is relevant as well. The Bible contains the word of God, and He only brings truth to His people. I deliver this message for one simple reason: Many people say the Bible is not relevant.

In his book, *The Relevance of the Prophets*, pages 14-17, R. B. Y. Scott, professor in the Department of Religion at Princeton University, offers his thesis that the prophets of Israel disclosed the reality and nature of our twentieth-century crisis when speaking about their own time. Our responsibility is an appropriate response to God. The Minor Prophets' strong faith commanded that Yahweh was, is and will always be the true Lord God. It was the fabric of this commanding faith that supported relevant prophecies with moral certainty and spiritual understanding for the people of Israel, the people of the twentieth century and for the people of all times. The prophets "are the contemporaries of every generation because the truth they declared is permanently valid (Ibid, p. 15)."

These great prophets of Almighty God expressed a tremendous concern for the social conditions and public issues that mark a spiritual crisis; human situations and moral issues were ignored. Their own time was brought under severe question and was eventually judged by God, just as He continues to do today. The human situations and moral issues of the twentieth century, and now going into the twenty-first century, are still being ignored.

- Children are fatally shooting other children.
- Generation X (children from 1965 through 1975) is vindictively conning senior citizens out of their life savings.
- Certain "Christian" organizations terrorize those people who are racially diverse.
- A community is no longer free to walk outside at night.
- People driving on the highway are fatally shot for apparently only looking at their assailant.

This list continues. The bad guys are protected under their "civil rights" while all the victims are usually forgotten by the judicial system. Herein is the marking of a spiritual crisis for us today. What can be learned from the Minor Prophets to bring us hope?

We shall begin with Amos (760–746 B.C.), more popularly known as the "Burden-bearer," who stepped out of a shepherd's role to become one of God's first and greatest reformers. His insight into the contemporary conditions of his day, his indignation toward corruption, and his courage and devotion to God made him worthy of this special honor. Israel was politically and socially corrupt from the top to the bottom. Amos showed a "mirror" of evil and the judgment of doom that Israel would face in guilt and shame. The doom was for Israel and her neighboring nations as the following:

1. Amos described the negative and positive aspects toward their punishment—the mismanagement of land and that God had the right to judge them.
2. Men caused women to act like the "cows of Basham" (Amos 4:1) and therefore had to be punished.
3. God's anger wanted to exile Israel rather than accept her burnt offerings.
4. Amos' visions of doom.
5. The restoration of David's kingdom.

Much of Israel's sin can be evenly compared with the sin of Christians today. The Christian faith has standards for all members to obey, just like Amos reminded Israel. One of the basic rules is to love and serve God, which includes loving and serving other people. We can only demonstrate this love and service when we are committed to God and His people, when we remain loyal to God and His people, and when we learn why and how God made us in His image.

Some Christians do not take as God seriously as He does of Himself. They need to study the Book of Amos for a lesson on God's seriousness. This lack of seriousness was obvious to me as I observed many commanders in the US Army. They viewed chaplains as good-luck charms or would call the chaplain "a butler who comes to pour gravy." With more shame, they would schedule a worship service at the same time that a meal was given during a field exercise. It's shameful for Christians to express their need for God only when they feel it's important. Amos had nothing less to point out to Israel as a warning. God's anger toward Israel could easily be the same for the Christians of today.

Let us now consider Hosea during his time "in the prosperous days of the reign of Jeroboam II" (786–746 B.C.).[15] Hosea dealt with the decline of religion, morals and politics in the Northern Kingdom of Israel. Hosea's immediate horrified response was, "A vulture is over the house of the Lord" (Hosea 8:1). There were no legitimate kings in the country for Hosea, since they emerged from violence and rebellion. Hosea was primarily sent by God, not to announce doom but to effect a return and reconciliation (Hosea 14:1–3). He had two basic messages: (a) People can go astray into a very ridiculous life of sin, and (b) the power, grace and glory of God are clearly demonstrated.

Israel went into the very depths of sin by worshipping other gods and was compared with a common prostitute, represented by Hosea's wife, who left the Almighty God to serve Baalim (Hosea 2:13, 15). Hosea's children's names were symbols of God's judgment: Jezreel means, "God shall scatter"; Lo-Ruhamah means, "Not pitied"; and (c) Lo Ammi means, "Not my people." Later, after he rejects his prostitute wife, Hosea takes her back, symbolizing God's forgiving nature and His love and grace (Hosea 14:4–9). God's anger and profound compassion truly reflects His own dramatic tension about Israel. Her pride caused a very long delay before repentance, and God's deep love for Israel delayed a harsh judgment. This drama finally played out with a positive conclusion. Hosea's account is an incredible means of communicating the depth of God's love for His people. This message remains relevant for the twenty-first century and beyond.

Are Christians truly serving the Almighty God? Let us consider a few questionable examples. The Apostle Paul provides a window showing the useful time we may abuse (Ephesians 5:15–20). He warns against being foolish by excluding regular worship service attendance. Some Christians are known for talking business during a worship service. Politicians are known for confusing their allegiance between politics and God. The rich serve money and power rather than God (Matthew 19:20–22). Some people lust for abnormal sensual pleasures rather than properly loving their helpmate. There are many more examples of perversity that don't bring any glory to God. How our time is spent should be useful and acceptable to God Almighty. Hosea warned Israel how and why they lost their fellowship with God, just as he is warning us today. We were created to glorify God and not ourselves. We must wake up to the Bible since it still remains relevant in our own time.

We now come to the prophet Micah (735–686 B.C.), who was at the village of Moresheth-gath—a small town on the border of Judah and Philistia, 22 to 25 miles southwest of Jerusalem (Micah 1:1, 14). Micah was defined as a prophet for the poor and downtrodden. He had a "courageous and fearless spirit... [to challenge] the corrupted and heartlessness of inhuman rulers and time-serving religionists."[16] Micah chose to denounce the wrong of his day in the strongest language he knew. He was described as a man who possessed Amos's passion for justice and Hosea's heart for love. Micah summed up all his power: "But as for me, I am full of power by the spirit of the Lord, and of judgment, and of might, to declare unto Jacob his transgression, and to Israel his sin" (Micah 3:8). Micah stressed the holiness of the Lord and the righteousness of God's government. As long as God's people would do right, they would enjoy His favor and would not suffer punishment. Lives should demonstrate a spirit of humility toward God by recognizing one's brotherly relation to his fellows. Social injustices were sternly rebuked.

"Politics as usual" is now a cliche, and the situation is questionable at best. We often hear about people "losing their faith" in politics. What can be done to change this situation? Our nation needs politicians and judges that are under the reign of God's righteousness. They must raise themselves above the lust for power by using their authority appropriately. Their faith ought to command dignity and respect from the people they serve. Micah envisioned a worthy example as the Messianic Hope (Micah 5:2–15), and politicians would serve their constituents well by applying this example to themselves. Micah 7:1–5 clearly describes God's harsh judgment for total corruption. This warning includes the corruption of our politicians. They, too, must wake up to the Bible.

Our fourth prophet is Zephaniah, which means "Jehovah hides," or "Jehovah has hidden," or "treasured."[17] Scholars are not certain about Zephaniah's actual date for ministry, but perhaps we can accept 630 to 625 B.C. This date would have both Jeremiah and Zephaniah ministering during the same period. His ancestry could represent royal blood since King Hezekiah of Judah was identified as Zephaniah's great-great-grandfather. Jerusalem was his home, but we do not know anything concerning his occupation.

Zephaniah's prophecies most likely began during the rise of the Babylonian Empire and their westward threat. Josiah led Judah, but Zephaniah was not impressed over the so-called reforms and "good life" Josiah instigated. Zephaniah only saw nervousness, cruelty and corruption among the people.

> Social injustice and moral corruption appear to be widespread; luxury and extravagance are seen on every hand. The Baalim were still worshiped, and what worship was offered to Jehovah was little other than idolatry. The time was ripe for judgment.[18]

Zephaniah offered repentance for the people and God's grace of salvation as the formula for a bright new beginning and future.

Perhaps the downfall for Israel was that her hopes were too high; they eventually became empty. The people never recognized the subtlety of it all, and God's warnings through His prophets were never heard as well. Their self-interests were a stumbling block for them. Yes, they had a good life of luxury and extravagance. But corruption foamed at the top and the fermentation of complacency destroyed Israel's selfishness. Zephaniah 3:1–7 warns Jerusalem that God's judgment will be commensurate with the heathen actions of her inhabitants. The remnant of God's people finally rejoiced over God being in their midst.

Christians of today are not exempt from falling into the self-interest trap. God truly knows our limitations and will always guide us to a realistic hope. I never heard or read that God rejects luxury for His people, but being extravagant and complacent about wealth will lead to corruption.[19] Zephaniah had an obvious concern for God's people, and his words are most assuredly relevant for today. Let us, therefore, wake up to the Bible.

The fifth prophet is Nahum (663–612 B.C.), which means "Consolation," or "Consoler."[20] His name is symbolic of his mission to comfort the oppressed and afflicted people of Judah. His birthplace is somewhat of an enigma for scholars, but let us be happy with Judah or southern Palestine. We also have no idea about his occupation.

Nahum was a prophet with just a single theme: The city of Nineveh will fall from destruction because of its great sin and dreadful people. He defined them as having outrageously wicked and cruel minds. The Assyrian rulers built their empire by greed and blood—an ultimate sacrifice for the victims. The rulers' idolatrous behavior emphasized a life of materialism, apathy and sensuous pleasure. The population was made up of foreigners who were drawn by trade and wealth. Trade and commerce became the only means to hold the city together and also eventually became the reason it broke apart. The whole milieu of oppression and affliction demanded a word from God, Who found a voice through Nahum and revealed the eternal principle of Himself: He commands righteousness and truth before giving His blessing of survival.

Can one person deny that all of these examples of evil exist in America? If not, then Prophet Nahum's voice needs to be heard today as well. Once again, we can clearly see markings of a spiritual crisis for America and a desperate need for hope from our Lord and Savior. Nahum is truly relevant to us today.

Our sixth prophet is Habakkuk (612–600 B.C.), which means "ardent embrace." Farrar prefers "embraced" or "pressed to the heart." Geikie says, "His name, as Luther well puts it, speaks as one who took his nation to his heart, comforted it and held it up, as one embraces and presses to his bosom a poor weeping child, calming and consoling it with good hope—if God so will." Ibid. p. 271. Scholars know nothing about Habakkuk's occupation and only the content of this Old Testament book could imply Habakkuk's home was Jerusalem. Habakkuk's background was very much like Zephaniah's, but with a few differences. Jehoahaz, son of King Josiah, was made king after the death of his father at Megiddo. King Jehoahaz ruled for only three months, but was just as cruel as his father. Eliakim, the brother of Jehoahaz, became king and ruled for 11 years. His reign was as equally wicked as his father's and brother's were.

Habakkuk never took God's message to the people but, rather, took all complaints of the people to God. All the lawlessness and injustices in Judah and Jerusalem and the rising power of Babylon most likely had a negative impact on Habakkuk's faith, and he took his problem of faith to God. It made Habakkuk more perplexed when God used the Chaldean people, who were more wicked and ruthless than Judah, as a punishment. Although perplexed, Habakkuk finally studied his people's history and learned God's judgments were for the salvation of His people. This cleared up his problem and allowed his faith to reach its peak when he expressed the principle which God gave him: "The righteous shall live by faith" (Habakkuk 2:4). The destiny of all nations is in God's hand; God might tolerate the wicked people, but they must ultimately receive their just recompense.

The eternal lessons we learned from Habakkuk are:

1. Our faithfulness to God will guarantee a place of permanence that will endure forever.
2. The righteous must be patient to survive all the tyranny and arrogance until the tyrants self-destruct.
3. Suffering brings discipline, whether as an individual (Job's lesson) or as a nation.
4. All God's people will grow spiritually when they learn the lessons of perplexity and they absolutely trust in God.

Although there are twelve Minor Prophets, I chose to rely on these six to represent the twelve. I encourage further study for those who might have gained a desire to learn more about them—Obadiah, Joel, Jonah, Haggai, Zechariah and Malachi. A marking of a spiritual crisis occurred during the time of these prophets and continues today. What will you do about it? Ours is not to reason why, but to do or die. May God's grace and mercy be with us all. Amen.

Addendum Two

The Kingdom of God and Heaven

The central theme in the message and ministry of Jesus was the kingdom of God. In place of the word God was occasionally heaven. I shall attempt to clarify the reason for using heaven as we move along.

Both Jesus and John the Baptist, a cousin of Jesus, began their ministry, "Repent ye; for the kingdom of heaven is at hand" (Matthew 3:2; 4:17). In another example, Jesus defined his mission as, "I must preach the good news of the kingdom of God to other cities also: for I was sent for this purpose." (Luke 4:43). Although our first example used the word heaven to describe the kingdom, the second example used the word God. Both mean the same thing in the sense that the kingdom, indeed, belongs only to God. Another difference for using God or heaven is in relationship to the Almighty Heavenly Father; God is usually written when the Bible refers to Jesus or the Holy Spirit.

Why should the word God, as any member of the Godhead, be used for the statement: "The kingdom of God actively works in our lives"? The kingdom of God ministers to a person who is filled with confusion, hate, distrust, etc., by removing those negative feelings and filling that person with love, an overwhelming trust in Christ, a clear mind and many other blessings. A whole new outlook on life is created for that person. Although Christ and the Holy Spirit performed this mission, the Almighty Heavenly Father willed it to happen. Therefore, we can say that the kingdom of heaven was "at hand" for that person.

Let us now move on with a more definitive study of two biblical problems that need resolution.

The Basic Meaning of the Kingdom of Heaven

The word heaven should have a significant meaning for us when we learn it appears 33 times in the New Testament alone. Why do I make this claim? We all agree that the word baptize has a very significant meaning, but it appears only 23 times in the New Testament. Its past tense, baptized, appears 40 times. I further contend that most people do not understand the meaning of heaven equally well as they do the word baptize. I want to offer you an opportunity to learn more about the use of heaven.

Our gratitude should go to the Judaic teachings, which can be found in any Old Testament study. Our study is consistent with their sensitivity of applying a cautious use of the word Yahweh. It was too sacred for any person even to pronounce. They would rather use such words as Adonai or Eloheim when addressing God. Perhaps two examples will assist the learning process.

A. "For the kingdom of heaven is at hand" (Matthew 3:2). Most people during this period understood that the Almighty Heavenly Father was sending a king to rule on earth. Since the verbal use of Yahweh was not permitted, the word heaven was used, denoting that the Heavenly Father willed an earthly Davidic kingdom to include political rule. Dr. George Eldon Ladd described the kingdom of God as it relates to Jesus: "The kingdom of God is the sovereign rule of God manifested in the person and work of Christ, creating a people over whom he reigns, and issuing in a realm or realms in which the power and blessings of his reigns are realized."[21] Only the Heavenly Father has supreme authority to manifest sovereign rule by willing it to happen through the person and work of his only begotten son, Jesus the Christ.

B. The prodigal son decided he sinned against heaven / God (Luke 15:21) and Jesus asked the people where baptism came from: heaven (God) or men (Matthew 21:25). Both Scriptures refer to the Almighty Heavenly Father. I therefore use heaven anytime our Heavenly Father rules /wills on something. Perhaps we can all understand now why Jesus used the word *heaven* more than *God*. Jesus is God but not the Almighty Heavenly Father. We must now consider our second biblical problem.

The Basic Meaning of the Kingdom of God

Jesus would say "kingdom of God," but what exactly did He mean? He apparently never defined what he meant. We can only speculate from the messages of Jesus in light of his personality and entire ministry. Since Jesus is the Son of the Heavenly Father, we can only assume that Jesus was also given by his Father the sovereign authority to rule in this kingdom. His mission was to educate people about the kingdom of God. Perhaps his first lesson was telling the people that all authority of this kingdom was turned over to him. Matthew 4:10 explains: "Jesus said to him, 'Away with you, Satan! For it is written, Worship the Lord your God, and serve only him.'" Satan somehow thought he could convince Jesus that all the kingdoms of the world were his to give. The reverse was true; Jesus already had sovereign authority over a kingdom that ruled the whole world and the entire universe. We shall learn more about how Jesus explained the kingdom and how He and the Holy Spirit share in the rule as well.

The word heaven is used any time one is referring to the Almighty Heavenly Father and what He wills. We also learned that Jesus used the term kingdom of heaven more than kingdom of God. Let us now store all of this information in our minds while we go on a long journey of life experiences. There is much more to learn about how, when, what and where the kingdom of heaven / God operates.

LIFE EXPERIENCE

Deliverance and the Kingdom

We begin with the Judaic history, when Adam and Eve lived on earth in peace and harmony until their first sin occurred by taking the forbidden fruit. Their sin was motivated by their mutual, innate disregard for Almighty God's authority. They ate the forbidden fruit and suddenly realized their nakedness. God had to search for Adam and Eve to find them because they hid from their shame. God judged their sin by:

1. Exiling them from the Garden of Eden.
2. Eve would endure pain in childbearing.
3. Adam would endure hard labor for bread to eat.
4. Both would die and return to the ground.

Most theologians agree that God's people began offering up their prayers of repentance after Adam and Eve were exiled. The Almighty Heavenly Father always offered deliverance from further judgment. God wants His people to experience peace, love and joy, rather than living in sin. This was Almighty God's greatest reason for sending Christ into the world: To deliver (save) people from sin and offer eternal life. This kingdom of heaven acts with power, exercising sovereignty for the defeat of Satan (given free will by the Almighty God) and the restoration of human society to its proper relationship of obedience to the will of the Almighty God. All evil forces against God will also be frustrated by God (I Corinthians 15:25). Ultimately and theologically, Almighty God's final plan is to deliver His people from sin and, through the biblical promise of eternal life, symbolically restore them back to the Garden of Eden.

The Last Days and the Kingdom

Perhaps it is appropriate to consider when God's people will experience what are called the Last Days. The Greek word for this concept is eschatos /eschata; an English word is eschatology from a doctrine of the "last things", or for some theologians— "the absolute end of the world."–Bakers Dictionary of Theology, p. 187. A Hebrew biblical usage in the LXX, a Greek translation from Hebrew, is, "En tais eschatais hemerais"—the last, or latter, days. The Hebrew word is *Be'aharit Hayyamin*. Many people view this as an individual human experience, but others say this refers to the world's last existence. Perhaps it will be more appropriate to use this word eschatology in the sense that God's redemptive history is now being consummated.[22] There is no absolute knowledge of whether the study is about human history or the world's existence. One can be absolutely sure that the kingdom operates during the Last Days. The kingdom reigns through all ages and it will not have its completion until our Lord comes again. Almighty God's sovereignty over creation—in His seasonal gifts of fertility and harvest and in His redemptive plan for His people—will be fully consummated during the manifestation of Christ's presence. Our Lord's redemptive work will come to a close and, "The creation itself will be set free from its bondage to decay and will obtain the freedom of the glory of the children of God" (Romans 8:21). Amen.

Old Testament Eschatology

The individual eschatology in the Old Testament subscribed to an existence after death, but Scriptures are rather shadowy at best. You will at least note the word Sheol, which is a vast underworld region where the dead dwell together as shades and their former status and character has little account. The dead do not sing praises of God in Sheol (Psalms 88:10 ff.; Isaiah 39:18). One of the most popular thoughts claimed that Sheol was not in Yahweh's reigning kingdom. However, we can read that a person who spent all his/her life walking with God can indeed have God's companionship in death (Psalms 139:8). Other than perhaps on a national level (Ezekiel 37:11; & Isaiah 26:19), there is also the notion of a resurrection for individuals, perhaps in the Last Days (Daniel 12:2).

World Eschatology

World eschatology in the OT is closely related to "the day of the Lord" (Amos 5:18–20). This particular day would be for Yahweh's judgment against the ungodly—especially the unrighteous among God's chosen people. There is an apparent disparity between what was actual and ideal. It was once said that on the day of Yahweh, His righteous kingship would be universally acknowledged and the earth would be filled with "the knowledge of the Lord" (Isaiah 11:9 cf. Habakkuk 2:14). It was believed that the house of David represented the divine kingship on earth. A coming king would emerge for the Almighty God to fulfill all the bright promises that had been made to David.[23] Hence, the Jews began hoping for their Davidic Messiah. That person would ascend this Davidic throne as Almighty God's permanent "Vicar."

Book of Daniel

The Book of Daniel offers us another interpretation of the Last Days. There was an apparent belief that Almighty God never abdicated His kingship over His people and that various pagan rulers attained power only as long as Almighty God permits. The pagan kingdom would later end at the time when:

> One like a human being comes with the clouds of heaven. And he came to the Ancient One and was presented before him. To him was given dominion and glory and kingship, that all peoples, nations, and languages should serve him. (Daniel 7:13–14a)

We later learn how Daniel's vision is fulfilled (Daniel 7:22) when the kingdom of God was present during the ministry of Jesus. The OT hopes and promises were finally fulfilled in Jesus.[24] To enter the kingdom of God is to enter into a present life of joy, peace and inner strength over pain, along with a hope for eternal life. Jesus ultimately becomes in "Himself the fulfillment of the hope of the people of God, the 'Amen' to all God's promises" at a time we call the Last Days.[25]

Present Reality and the Kingdom

We have briefly explored the concepts of deliverance and the Last Days, and now we are going to build upon them. They will become even clearer as we study the kingdom of God in light of its present reality.

Childhood serves as a learning experience that appropriately informs us what should occur when we perform a specific function. I learned the value of forgiveness by asking my parents for their forgiveness of my bad conduct as a child. The opposite of this "voluntary" gathering of knowledge was the "involuntary" punishment I received if I refused to quit my bad conduct. Either way, I learned. Childhood also includes moments when neighborhood children share their personal experiences with their parents. Eventually we got the big picture about how life was really supposed to be. Hence, we experienced a childlike present reality.

Likewise, if we consider the OT period as the childhood of God's people, Almighty God represents a parent to His children. Beginning with the bad conduct of Adam and Eve and continuing with all of those who followed, there are plenty of examples of the knowledge of good and evil and forgiveness. Church history taught that the "children" got some information from their neighbors—the Persian Zoroastrians. We have the apocalyptic writings that reveal this account in history—Apocryphal Book of Enoch, Baruch, etc. Such lessons on good and evil were clearly defined as the "day of ultimate reckoning, separation and regeneration, when evil would be burned up in purifying fire and the 'desired dominion' of good would be established."[26] The "children" of Israel truly learned how to apply these lessons to their present reality. The kingdom of God operates very much the same for our present reality today.

Redemption and the Kingdom

The kingdom of God is present in God's redemptive activity. The mission of Jesus is to break the power of evil and bring people the blessings of our Lord's rule. Beginning with his ministry on earth and going on to our present day, the activities of God's kingdom can be viewed, along with many others, as the present time. The theologian Jurgen Moltmann emphasized the present time in his book, Religion, Revolution and the Future. His thesis is only one concept on the view of present time. I highly recommend his book, along with any others who have written similar viewpoints.

Our present time is filled with two opposing forces—good and evil. Although the Heavenly Father is ultimately in supreme control, Satan has been given free will by the Father to oppose good in any way he chooses. On the other hand, Jesus has been given authority over Satan for all time to redeem God's people.[26] This remains active during the present time and will come to an end when God's redemptive activities become the final winner of the Last Days.

Powers of the Kingdom

The kingdom of God is present with dynamic power. We not only experience God's redemptive activities in the present time as a reality, but we also witness it. Perhaps the following examples of this gave cause for John the Baptist to question Jesus' legitimacy. John challenged whether or not Jesus was the Messiah and even sent delegations to make sure. We must keep in mind that John, too, believed in Daniel's Davidic kingship theory. All of Jesus' activities began illuminating the fact that Jesus would reign over a spiritual kingdom, which did not agree with John's interpretation of Daniel's vision. But Jesus' reply satisfied John the Baptist (Matthew 11:2–19; Luke 7:18–35).

Let us now consider a few examples of divine dynamic power in the kingdom of God. These theological points should be preceded by explaining that God's faithful will see the unfaithful change, and many of those people will enter the kingdom of God during the troubled times. Witnessing and experiencing such dynamic power in action represents the effect of our redemption caused by the kingdom of God.

1. A man with an unclean spirit is healed (Mark 1:21–28).
2. Simon's mother-in-law is healed (Matthew 8:14–17; Mark 1:29–34).
3. A leper man is healed (Matthew 8:1–4; Mark 1:40–45).
4. A paralytic is healed (Matthew 9:2–8; Mark 2:1–12).
5. A deaf man is healed (Isaiah 35:5–6; Mark 7:31–37).
6. A tax collector experiences a change (Mark 2:13–17).

Jesus told the people in the synagogue that everyone could experience this power (Luke 4:16–21). Sometimes a person might have an urgent feeling to seize God's offer of salvation; that is truly a moment of present reality.

The Kingdom's Completion

Our resource for God's completion of His kingdom is found in Matthew 24:1–51. We must be alert whenever Jesus shifts between issues of the present age and the age to come.

Our Responsibilities

Jesus taught about our responsibilities. Matthew 24 is an awesome scripture to grasp intellectually. I cannot begin to speculate on the imagery of God's kingdom coming to its completion. The following may not satisfy our natural quest for definitive knowledge on the subject, but it may help to gain some understanding.

At any given moment during the day, afternoon or evening, the radio may burst out with alarming news: War! All of Egypt, Saudi Arabia, Jordan, Syria, Iraq and Kuwait; the horrors of war that go beyond any imagination begin. The announcer gives incredible details of numerous fatalities. One needs to stop for a moment and reflect: What does this mean for the rest of the world? Would you think of Matthew 24:6, "And you will hear of wars and rumors of wars; see that you are not alarmed...." I hardly believe you would. Jesus went on to say, "Nations will rise against nations, and kingdom against kingdom, and there will be famines and earthquakes in various places: all this is but the beginning of the birthpangs." Jesus was preparing us for the completion of God's kingdom—the Last Days. God wants His people to remain faithful to Him and truly believe that He will never forsake them. This is our responsibility.

I would like to speculate on another image of God's kingdom coming to completion. The date could be today or even two months from today. I want you to imagine that a soldier in the Iraqi Army caught me. This could happen since I am still obligated to the US Army when another world war breaks out. I would not only be arrested but also tortured and put to death. Jesus promised that I would be saved if I would endure and remain faithful to God to the end. He describes this message as the "good news of the kingdom." Jesus claimed this good news must "be proclaimed throughout the world, as a testimony to all nations; and then the end will come." He wants us to realize that all suffering that comes from being associated with Jesus—being hated, falsely accused and led astray by false prophets—will be allowed. The Heavenly Father has His own divine reason for allowing Satan to frustrate His redemptive plan. Jesus even spoke more definitively about greater tribulations for God's "elected people" to endure (Matthew 24:14–28). Since the intensity of this tribulation would be too great for any person to endure and still remain faithful, Jesus promised that His Father would shorten the period of persecution for the sake of His people.

We find a comparative example of persecution in Daniel 11:31. Theologians refer to Antiochus Epiphanes as one who waged terrible persecutions against Israel in 168 B.C. If he had been successful, he would have obliterated the distinctive character of the Jewish nation and thus frustrated God's redemptive purpose.[28] Another example is found in Luke 21:20–24 that implies desolation for the people of Jerusalem similar to that predicted for the Last Days. Each of these examples serve as historical lessons to be learned.

Jesus wants us to warn others about the tribulations coming during the Last Days. This message is considered to be the good news. God's people have the responsibility of proclaiming this good news about the kingdom of God, which operates now and in the Last Days with the Son of Man.

The Second Coming

Jesus favored the title, Son of Man, since it adequately described His mission and Messianic person. Oddly, it was also a title that was never intended for use by the Christian church. The church fathers accepted the phrase to refer primarily to the humanity of the incarnate Son of God. Perhaps a brief review of biblical history will better serve as an explanation.

The Old Testament Account

I was able to find three contexts for the Son of Man:

1. It was frequently used as a synonym for man (Numbers 23:19; Psalm 144:3).
2. It was used by God more than 80 times as a name for the prophet Ezekiel (Ezekiel 2:1, 3, 6, 8; 3:1, 3, 4, etc.).
3. It was used in Daniel 7:13–14 to describe his vision of an apocalyptic personage.

Many modern scholars interpret this name as a representation of the saints of God—whether people or angels.[29] Others understand it as a heavenly Messiah that represents the people and brings God's kingdom to its realization on earth.[30]

THE APOCRYPHAL LITERATURE

Concerning the term Son of Man, scholars need to resolve the disparity that seemingly exists between the Jewish interpretation of Daniel 7 (about 100 BC), how the Apocryphal Book of Enoch uses it and Jesus' own reference to it in Matthew 26:64. The Book of Enoch contains greater detail about the Son of Man than the Book of Daniel; Enoch describes the Son of Man as a superhuman, if not a superangelic being, that comes to earth, Messiah-like, to judge God's people and inaugurate the kingdom of God. That kingdom would not be, therefore, an earthly political kingdom as found in the Psalms. There is no clear documentation on how an earthly political kingdom became included in Jewish teachings. There is also no clear explanation of why the vision of the Son of Man coming on the clouds of heaven is mentioned in Daniel 7 and Matthew 26 but *not* in Enoch 45, 55 or 58. So, we maintain better company if we stick with Jesus' use of the term *Son of Man*.

JESUS AND THE SON OF MAN

Jesus taught that the term *Son of Man* relates to Himself as the expected Messiah. We already learned how these two terms, *Son of Man* and *Messiah*, refer to the same person. Jesus made it clear that He was indeed that person. Jesus also taught how the Son of Man functions:

1. This Messianic office gives Jesus the authority to forgive sins (Matthew 9:5–6; Mark 2:10).
2. The Son of Man is Lord over the Sabbath (Mark 2:27–28) and, therefore, has authority to regulate the interpretation of how to use the Sabbath day.

3. The Son of Man was not only to endure *humiliation* and *suffering* (Mark 9:12, 31; 10:45), but He would also be the Son of Man in *glory* (Mark 13:26–27; Luke 17:24).

The glorious return of Jesus as the Christ will cause (a) the nation to mourn, (b) it will strike terror in the hearts of many people, and (c) the elect from God will know that the final judgment is about to break out.

The Last Days

We have the Gospel of Matthew 24:32–51 as our warning from Jesus about the Last Days. Although He warned us, Jesus still claimed that people would not be any more aware of the coming of the Son of Man than those people during Noah's time. Jesus said we ought to be aware of His coming just as we are aware of the summer being near when the fig tree begins to grow leaves. The Son of Man will come when we don't expect him. This ought to be a fair warning, but are we going to be ready? How many among us will truly be ready? Are we going to be like those during the days of Noah? The most important way to ensure readiness is by *accepting* the righteousness of God and by letting Him fill your total being.

Divine Righteousness and the Kingdom

The kingdom of God operates in the divine righteousness of Jesus and the Holy Spirit. Their righteousness is ushered into the lives of people who bear out this divine intervention through their *actions* and *behaviors*. A classic example is the person who insists on the *fair* and *just* treatment of others. Most people use the Golden Rule as their guideline. Matthew 7 deals with proper behavior:

1. 7:1–5 commands us not to judge others.
2. 7:6 deals with profaning the Holy Spirit.
3. 7:7–11 deals with asking in prayer, searching your soul and going to Jesus.
4. 7:12 is the Golden Rule.
5. 7:13–14 describes a difficult life.
6. 7:15–20 explains how false prophets can cause us to sin.
7. 7:21–23 warns against self-deception.
8. 7:24–29 explains how one can effectively hear and do the words of Jesus.

Even though there are only a few examples of Christian behavior, most people would not successfully achieve them unless divine righteousness was given. These examples unequivocally represent the kingdom of God operating in our lives; it is our responsibility to announce this warning to all who will listen.

We have now defined *how* Jesus and the Holy Spirit offer us divine righteousness by the kingdom of God. Let us keep this definition in mind while we cover the importance of the OT Torah and the theological opinions of Jesus. Just as Matthew 7 describes a relationship between God and His people, and points on Christian behavior, our study of the Torah and the opinion of Jesus includes a *similar* relationship; there is a difference of interpretation between the Torah and Jesus' opinion.

The Importance of the Torah

Among its many instructions for conduct in life, the Torah is a collection of laws that deals specifically with the conduct for *holiness*, such as Leviticus 17–26 offers. One can say that righteousness has the same *motive for conduct* as holiness. This collection of scriptures has been called the Law of Holiness. Without these instructions, life tends to have no meaning for the Jew. Perhaps Christians should consider their own prayer life as being that important. The Torah has as much importance for the Jew as the skeleton does for the body. I once met a Jewish lawyer in the army who used that comparison when he explained why the Torah was important for him. This was how he hoped to achieve a righteous relationship with God. Jesus had a different theological opinion.

The Opinion of Jesus

Much of the process of reading, learning and obeying the Torah seemed like an outward theatrical exposition for Jesus. He credited the Jewish people with learning their lessons well, but how much affect did these lessons actually have? How much internal improvement in a person's soul occurred? Jesus felt that going *beyond* the conduct was more important. He knew the inner soul and life of a person.[31] It follows, then, that Jesus continues to know how the soul of a person will improve with righteous values, ethics, spiritual insight and commitment. He knows that these virtues go beyond a person's conduct.

Values

We cannot touch or smell value, but we are aware of it. There is enjoyment and high value in one of Piccaso's paintings. Why? Something occurs between the painting and the viewer. One's individual value for that painting directly depends on one's esthetical preference. One will therefore pay a corresponding commensurable price. We can view this phenomenon during auctions of famous celebrity estates.

This same principle of relativity applies to a person's faith in God. One's private value of faith is commensurable to the amount of trust and suffering being paid. Death would be the ultimate price paid for one's faith in God. Our freedom to worship in America did not come without bloodshed. Americans ought to be grateful to those soldiers who died on the battlefield ensuring that this freedom to worship could continue to be enjoyed by all. Jesus apparently felt similarly concerning faith in His Heavenly Father. This includes the cross and clearly goes beyond just reading, learning and obeying the Torah (Matthew 16:24–28).

Ethics

Jesus disapproved of all merchants who indulged themselves in the unethical practice of selling items outside the temple (Mark 11:15–19). His concern was for people to make appropriate ethical choices, and those merchants made bad choices. The temple only had one purpose and that was as a place for prayer. Jesus also had a problem with the church rulers, who did not always respect the prophets and obey God's will (Mark 12:1–12).

In the parable, Jesus represented the vineyard owner's son who would eventually be killed. Jesus warned the rulers that God would judge their hidden plot to kill. The other side of that parable was the lack of respect the renters had for the owner's share of the produce. The kind of unethical behavior did not appeal to Jesus, nor did His Heavenly Father approve. Jesus never spoke against wealth, but He did mention the way wages were given and received (Luke 3:12–14; Romans 6:20–23). Perhaps Jesus felt the Torah did not deal with the interaction of God and His people but only instructed people on how to live (Deuteronomy 33:8–11). Jesus taught that both were vital.

SPIRITUAL INSIGHT

Everyone has an independent understanding of the term *spiritual insight.*[32] Church doctrines tend to offer keen insights, but they are also easily confused with the Holy Scriptures. I contend that the same warning holds true for uninformed Christians who claim that God gave them spiritual messages. Church history has shown repeated danger in such activity. Christians are warned about false prophets and messages.[33] One obtains spiritual insight through a daily walk with God in prayer, Bible study, listening to God's voice, and being open for God's ministry (Psalms 23:4; John 8:12). Again, I warn against being careless by not carefully studying the Scriptures for the truth. Our Lord will never allow us to go too far off the course (John 14:1–7).

COMMITMENT

A solid commitment to the previously mentioned virtues is vitally important. One must believe in them with all of one's heart, soul and mind.[34] Talking about your faith is only a start, but putting your faith into action goes beyond reading, learning and obeying the Torah. People see the kingdom of God when you actively show God's righteousness strengthening your faith; your commitment is a living testimony. Let us, therefore, *shout out* how His righteousness has changed our lives.

The Church and the Kingdom

Where are the members for the kingdom of God? Was Jesus' ministry and His offer of this kingdom directed primarily at Israel? Did Jesus want to include the Gentiles? Did Jesus want to reform Israel, or did He anticipate a people to replace the rebellious people of Israel?

Since Jesus considered the Israelites as the "sons of the kingdom" (Matthew 8:12; RSV), one could conclude that Jesus had offered His kingdom primarily to Israel. The fact that their covenant relationship, religious background and all of their traditions were enmeshed with the Heavenly Father, the Jews seemed to be the people who would inherit this kingdom. Hence, this is the very reason Jesus addressed His ministry to the Jews *first* and sent His disciples with specific instructions to "Go nowhere among the Gentiles, and enter no town of the Samaritans, but go rather to the lost sheep of the house of Israel" (Matthew 10:5–6). It is interesting to make a notation of the word *lost*. The Greek root means *to perish*. In light of this, the Israelites were not lost, as such, but they were *perishing*. The religious leaders of that day were mishandling the people. Unless someone came to rescue them, they would perish. Jesus was the Someone who came to rescue the Israelites.

The context in which Jesus came to rescue the Israelites is the same for Christians. Jesus came first to build His church with the Israelites, and the Apostle Peter was given the key to the kingdom of Heaven (Matthew 16:18–20). Jesus apparently used the word *church* in reference to those people who will have access to the kingdom of Heaven. Given the word *Heaven*, we must conclude that Jesus was referring to His Heavenly Father, who ultimately reigns over Christ's church and yet *willed* Jesus to be the Head of the church. Also, we can further conclude that Christ's church is for the Jews first, and the Gentiles are heirs of His church. A gathering of people who were called out from the world through divine election by the Heavenly Father represents a church. This church is conceived on a local congregational level.[35] We can view Christ's church as being for the Jews first and then the Gentiles (Christians).

THE CHURCH FOR ISRAEL

The kingdom of Heaven reigns in the church for Israel. Jesus made three striking observations during His mission on earth of explaining how the kingdom of Heaven operated in the church for Israel.

1. **Jesus observed misunderstandings.** The issue of a *postponed* kingdom for Israel became an important element in a dispensational study on the Last Days. We already mentioned how the Jews confused the messages from the Apocryphal Book of Enoch (Daniel 7; Matthew 26). The Jews were looking for their new Davidic Messiah to rule as a permanent "Vicar." Jesus presented Himself as the Messiah but to rule over the *spiritual* kingdom of His church. Daniel's vision was indeed fulfilled by Jesus, but many Jews never accepted Him as the promised Messiah.

2. **Jesus observed rejection.** The church under the kingdom of Heaven will never lack people of enormous faith (Matthew 8:8–10). A few examples of rejection are recorded in Matthew 11:

a) 11:1–15 Jesus offered a choice to accept or reject John the Baptist as a representative of the spirit of Elijah. He was rejected.
b) 11:16–19 Both Jesus and John the Baptist offered the good news. It was rejected.
c) 11:20–24 Jesus warned the Israelites about God's judgment, but they did not repent.
d) 11:25–30 Jesus gave thanks to His Heavenly Father for the remnant—the "wise and understanding"—who were in the midst of suffering for the sake of the good news. They still accepted Jesus as the true Messiah.

While Israel as a nation rejected the kingdom, this remnant among the Israelites accepted it, along with the tax collectors and harlots who proved to be the true sons of the kingdom.

3. Jesus observed no final judgment for the Israelites. Jesus continued to warn the Israelites about God's judgment, but He never said the Heavenly Father had totally turned His back on them (Matthew 23:13–15). It is safe to conclude that the "ball" is now in Israel's "court", whether or not they will change their minds and hearts. As for Christ's followers, who are now considered to be Christians, the problem of misunderstanding still remains.

Christians and the Kingdom

The kingdom of heaven reigns for Christians. There are three implications that actually define Christ's church.

1. The church as a strong foundation. The church's foundation began with the Messiah, a true claim for all believers and one they are willing to die in support of. This becomes very important since it links with the OT prophecy in Daniel 7 and verifies Matthew 26. Secondly, Peter's confession in Matthew 16:16, "You are the Messiah, the Son of the living God," builds upon that foundation of legitimacy. Members today confess this same truth during each worship service.

Finally, the church will be stronger than death since it represents life eternal. In his book, *Common Fellowship*, H. Richard Niebuhr describes his faith while suffering in a WWII prison camp. Most people can hardly accept the imagery of a prison guard looking in the cell with a strong sense of power over the oppressed. Richard somehow reversed this imagery by looking out as though the guard was the oppressed in a cell. Richard never felt he had power over the guard, but rather, he had a great amount of divine love (agape love) for the guard. The church, in this regard, is stronger than death.

2. The church receives a key to the kingdom. All believers receive authority to enter the kingdom of heaven and Christ's church since Jesus gave the key to Peter (Matthew 16:19). This was also prophesied in Isaiah 22:22, "And I will place on his shoulder the key of the house of David; he shall open, and none shall shut; and he shall shut, and none shall open." No one has the right (the key) to take away Christ's church from any believer.

Jesus told the Pharisees and Scribes that they possessed the "key of knowledge" but never gave it to the people (Luke 11:52). The leaders had an obligation to give this key of knowledge, but they failed. I contend this is the very same key—if *not* the same in actuality, at the very least in symbolic terms—which Jesus passed on to Peter. We ought to take note of this important biblical lesson. All Christians need to confess Jesus as the Messiah, Son of the living God, and share the knowledge of His kingdom with all people.

3. The church serves as a fellowship of believers. This emphasis simply illustrates that the kingdom of God/Heaven involves people. The church is therefore people, the instruments of the kingdom, assisting God in accomplishing His work. The people's confession strengthens the foundation of Christ's church. His people most assuredly enjoy the key of knowledge that the Apostle Peter received from Jesus. We must always pray for wisdom to protect this awesome responsibility. Satan remains active and evil.

Conclusion

We learned how the kingdom of Heaven/God works in the church—whether originally through the Israelites or now through Christ's church. We also learned that Christ's church could easily make the same mistake the Israelites did by withholding the key of knowledge from God's people (Matthew 10:5–6). I contend Christ's church is not without sin; the Heavenly Father is now walking among His people through His Son and Holy Spirit to reveal such sins as complacency, greed, resentment, jealousy, arrogance, murder, etc. His judgment can be quite severe. We ought to be in repentant prayer for further redemption in Christ's church. Christians have the responsibility to warn against these sins and command the perishing sheep to seek the kingdom of God first.

The Lost Sheep and the Kingdom

The kingdom of God operates under three agendas.

1. **The Shepherd seeks any lost / perishing sheep** (Luke 15:1–7). Luke used this particular language to describe the scriptural references of Jesus as the Shepherd.[36] All the people understood a shepherd's authority and responsibility; accounting for the lost sheep is vital. Indeed, Jesus felt this level of concern for all the people—each one of us—perishing without salvation. Jesus offers *unconditional forgiveness* to all who believe in Him.

2. **The motives, incentives and desires of Jesus.** Jesus once described the extent to which we ought to love others as the Heavenly Father loves us. Having such love would make us perfect, as the Heavenly Father is perfect (Matthew 5:43–48). This is truly awesome. How should we understand this

great expectation from Jesus? We first need to understand that He is the subject and we are the objects of His motives, incentives and desires. Jesus seeks us out to offer redemption, peace of mind and perfection. We become perfect and receive those blessings only from his authority. We can then outwardly show perfect love from within us, since Jesus lives within us (Galatians 2:20). Perhaps there is no other reason that Jesus has been given the authority to seek the lost/perishing sheep. The kingdom of God, through the mission of Jesus, seeks us *first*.

3. **God's unconditional forgiveness.** All followers of God—Father, Son and Holy Spirit—are more fortunate than they might realize. A classic image of someone's response is like the dog that bites the hand that feeds it. And yet, the kingdom of God continues to seek them. These ungrateful people are offered several opportunities to experience God's merciful forgiveness. Jesus once compared all people with birds of the air. He claimed that if His Father provides for them, then how much more will the Father provide for His people since they have more value than birds (Matthew 6:25–26).

Although God chose us to receive His kingdom (2 Thessalonians 2:13–15), He also gave us the freedom to choose sin (Luke 10:38–42; Hebrews 11:26). These two options not only demonstrate God's unconditional love, mercy and forgiveness, but they also proclaim the good news. Many people choose sin, and their priorities have become confused. Let us consider some of them in the following:

1. They choose selfishness in all opportunities.

2. They choose profit over the safety and welfare of others.
3. The government spends more money on judicial rights for criminals than the next-to-nothing amount they spend for all the victims.

God's unconditional forgiveness even includes these three examples of sin. The Shepherd seeks the lost/perishing sheep and many hear His voice (Matthew 18:10–14; John 10:16). The sheep truly needs the Shepherd.

Why We Need the Kingdom

Jesus taught why people need the kingdom (Mark 4:24–34; 10:29–30). He asked a rather important question: "With what can we compare the kingdom of God?" (Mark 4:30). We know what the kingdom of God *is*, but what is it compared to? I contend God's kingdom is compared with *mysteries*.[37] Jesus taught that only God can reveal the mysteries of His kingdom, and His disciples know these mysteries; others would not understand even if they were told. These parables were a defense mechanism used by Jesus against untrustworthy people. Only the apostles who knew these mysteries were actually trustworthy stewards of them. They, therefore, had to be cautious with their knowledge.

Extending this even further, we need to consider the Apostle Paul's accounts in 1 Corinthians 13 and 14. He mentioned that *love* had far more value than prophetic powers or the understanding of mysteries. Secondly, Paul claimed that speaking in unknown tongues was actually a communication with God concerning His mysteries. We should conclude from these scriptures that the kingdom of God contains mysteries that only God has the authority to reveal. The disciples protected their meanings as trustworthy stewards, and only God decides the time when His mysteries are revealed. Perhaps Jesus asked His disciples what they would compare God's kingdom to, so they would clearly understand that God's people need His kingdom. Most people are intrigued with mysteries, but such mysteries could strike people with fear as well.

1. **Satan is the main cause of fear.** The Apostle Paul tells us in 2 Corinthians 4:4 that Satan is the "god of this age." This "god" goes by two names: Satan (evil one) and devil (slanderer or accuser). His subordinates is the prince of demons, Beelzebub, and others (Mark 3:22).

We already claimed that Christians are the "sons of God" when being in bondage to Christ.[38] Those who are in satanic bondage (Luke 13:16) are called the "sons of Satan/evil one" (Matthew 13:38–39). People who are possessed by demons suffer immensely (Mark 5:3–5). Many contemporary psychiatrists and psychologists have proven that they often misunderstand this truth by diagnosing such conditions as either chemical or mental disorders. I agree that a good diagnosis is complicated, but one cannot just totally dismiss demonic possession. One scripture offers the best way to diagnose and treat such a condition. Mark 1:21–28 tells a story of a demon-possession man who does not end up personally suffering, but Jesus actually confronts the demons (Mark 1:24). They not only called out to Jesus by name, but they also asked whether Jesus came to destroy them. Such a dialogue between Jesus and the demons is overwhelming evidence that demons communicate with people. However, most people have a basic need for more proof. The exorcist or counselor should always have a few people to witness the event, in light of many a "doubting Thomas." Nothing less is done at any psychiatric clinic.

2. **People can become victims of fear.** Satan attacks people to further his bitter revenge toward God (Isaiah 14:12–14; Ezekiel 28:12–15). It is because of his fallen relationship that we are now tossed about like Ping-Pong balls. We are indeed in the middle of this intense battle as innocent victims with the most to lose. Our sins can range from very minor offenses on up to eternal damnation. Our salvation in this situation is to recognize that we need the kingdom of God.

3. **Sin is the object of fear.** We must understand that sin caused Satan to fall from God's grace, and sin is the only reason for us to fall from God's grace as well. Satan only knows sin, and he wants people to suffer in hell with him. Consider this brief philosophical comment.

Ezekiel 28:11–16 describes Satan as being perfect, wise, beautiful and one who simply "had it made" in the Garden of Eden. He was most likely jealous when God created Adam and Eve. Since Satan could not remain blameless, he was cast out of Heaven as a profane thing. His jealousy, most likely, did not allow Adam and Eve to remain in the Garden of Eden. This is similar to the state of troubled husbands who are jealous of their wives. The husband resents a divorce and, therefore, would never allow his wife to live with another man. If the husband decides to kill himself, he must kill his wife first. Satan portrayed this kind of jealousy, but with a slight twist: Since Satan couldn't kill God, his next option was to destroy eternal peace in the Garden of Eden for Adam and Eve.

Although we can conclude that these three points on fear have a devastating effect on us, we must also remember them as reasons for needing the kingdom of God. Without this understanding and acceptance, we will not understand *why* we must seek the kingdom first.

Seeking the Kingdom First

Salvation is not given unless we first seek the kingdom (Matthew 6:24–34). Faith is the driving force in seeking the kingdom of God (Matthew 17:14–21). We already established the two answers for how the kingdom operates among the lost /perishing sheep: (a) the Shepherd seeks them, and (b) the people need God's kingdom to maintain a stable and protective life.

1. Faith is the driving force in seeking God's kingdom. Jesus was quite disappointed with His disciples (Matthew 17:14–21). Their lack of faith in the attempt of healing the epileptic boy had less importance for Jesus than His disciples' lack of faith in the reigning powers of God's kingdom. The ultimate process of seeking His kingdom first requires faith in His kingdom. The disciples apparently did not have it. The healing in this situation came from the reigning powers of God's kingdom and *not* the disciples' faith in having the power of healing. Jesus knew His time on earth was getting shorter, and He must have wondered how much longer it would take His disciples to learn about the kingdom. The Scriptures are not very clear about the disciples' lack of faith until their response to Jesus' crucifixion:

- Judas betrayed Jesus (Mark 14:10–11).

- All the disciples deserted and scattered like sheep (Mark 14:26–27).
- Peter denied Jesus (Mark 14:66–72).

We must conclude from these examples that these disciples never developed a strong faith in God's kingdom until *after* the resurrection of Jesus. I personally do not believe anyone in this world today would have responded any different than these disciples. After all, they were ordinary men who were chosen by Jesus to do an extraordinary mission for Almighty God. Psalms 86 spoke well of these disciples. King David prayed as one who trusted in the good and forgiving God, Who abounds in steadfast love for all who call on Him. David, along with these disciples, firmly believed God would remain faithful in His love for them, even as they developed their faith.

2. **Jesus warned against trying to serve both God and wealth** (Matthew 6:24). Why? It should go without saying that Jesus meant it when He commanded: "But seek first the kingdom of God and His righteousness, and all these things will be given to you as well" (6:33). Jesus wanted His disciples to have this same faith when they conducted a ministry of healing. Faith must remain the same for us when we have wealth or when we live on a meager income. All people are equal in the eyes of God Almighty and, therefore, have equal opportunity to receive the kingdom of God. The Apostle Paul would say that all people begin at the same starting line in the race of life (1 Corinthians 9:24).

I might quickly add that his main point here was to be competitive, but it does not preclude the image of everyone forming equally at the starting line of life. We begin and finish the race together and as equals. Our faith is the driving force that enables us to finish this race. We are ultimately placing Jesus first in our lives when we seek His kingdom first. We ought to consider His will whenever we plan on anything.

Parables of the Kingdom

A parable contains a realistic story in familiar language that allegorizes a specific truth about the kingdom of God (Matthew 21:33–43; Mark 4:10–12). We already compared parables to God's mysteries, which only He reveals. Jesus used a series of short parables to teach a single truth, and He used one parable to teach a single truth as well. Jesus focused on fruits to show evidence of His sovereign rule within God's kingdom (Matthew 21:33–43). He gave evidence of God's greatness, power, mercy and righteousness and proved Christ's existence.

Perhaps one unquestionable example is the growth of our faith. I will use the artichoke to allegorize faith. I once purchased artichoke seeds to plant in my back yard. It began with a tiny plant but soon grew 6 to 7 feet tall. I had no doubt that I would have artichokes. In fact, I could hardly get rid of them. No one would doubt the *evidence* of their own growth as well. Our faith can easily show evidence like my artichoke. It is very difficult for other people to get rid of your strong faith.

The Evidence of Fruit

The evidence of fruit is witnessed through God's sovereign rule (Matthew 21:33–43). We must learn that we are simply managers of all God gave us in life. The parable of the landowner, who planted a vineyard, built a fence, dug a winepress and built a watchtower, represents God Who eventually sent His Son after such wicked tenants that caused His servants harm. The tenants then killed the landowner's son, who actually represents Jesus. The whole scenario is a description of how the people of Israel rejected Jesus and later crucified Him. All this did not happen by chance; God's sovereign rule actively worked in the life of Jesus.

This parable also revealed these other fruits:

1. A person's freedom to reject God.
2. People have the responsibility for their choice in life.
3. The kingdom of God is given to those people who produce fruit.

Single-Truth Parables

A parable with short stories will still have a single truth to teach (Matthew 13:24–50). The single truth in all of these short stories demonstrates *how* God reigns in His kingdom. God's judgment will be harsh for those who are evil and a blessing for those who are good. Within these short stories (a) weeds refer to evil and wheat refers to good; (b) mustard seeds refer to the greatest shrubs; (c) yeast refers to the growth of our faith and all that is acceptable by God; and (d) the kingdom of heaven and faith are described as hidden treasures. We already compared parables with mysteries, but the use of secrets will also be acceptable here.

Hidden Secret

A parable has a hidden secret that only God reveals (Daniel 2:28; Romans 16:25–26). We begin with Daniel's vision of the Last Days: "There is a God in Heaven Who reveals mysteries, and has made known to King Nebuchadnezzer what will be in the latter days." Hence, we should now notice God's hidden purposes being announced through the king's dream, which were later interpreted by Daniel. In substitution for an earthly kingdom of man, Daniel told the king that the heavenly kingdom of God would come. The word used in the New Testament has more significance and is further developed in Daniel's prophecy: "Now to Him Who is able to strengthen you according to my gospel and the preaching of Jesus Christ, according to the revelation of the mysteries which was kept secret for all ages, but is now disclosed and through the prophetic writings is made known to all nations, according to the command of the eternal God, to bring about the obedience of faith" (Romans 16:25–26). Paul proclaimed that God's mysteries are no longer kept a secret from the trustworthy people of God. His people will indeed hear. God's mysteries were once hidden in the mind of God, but now are being revealed by Him. Jesus, as the Son of God, was given authority to reveal them. Jesus came to clarify the meaning, mission and power of the kingdom of God. The parables were an effective mechanism for Jesus to communicate this kingdom.

A Mission for His People

Mission is a familiar word for all of us. We who served in the military know it so well. The word also is used in the Department of Veterans Affairs, or any other work place as well. Although not explicitly used, the descriptions of missions are found at least thirty-one times in the Bible. People obviously found a mission essential to survive, succeed and be victorious. Our reason for now is to explain how the kingdom operates as a mission for His people.

We begin by keeping in mind that God's kingdom is viewed in the sense of action. It is no longer viewed as a noun, but as a verb form. We say, "God is actively at work in the world." He is at work wherever His people are feeding the poor, building a shelter for the homeless, defending victims from evil intentions, visiting the sick, supporting a someone's loss, celebrating a person's victory and much more. The kingdom has no boundaries and it is not partial to any one person, ideology, theology or geography. God has plenty of missions for those who accept His calling.

Luke 10:2 says, "The harvest is plentiful, but the laborers are few." I suspect that most people already know that only a few people ever accept God's calling. This fact was true 2000 years ago and remains the same today. The Bible claims that this fact will not change in the future. We who accepted God's calling most likely feel overwhelmed, but we must go on! God's people must remember their callings, commitments and that we possess God's grace to complete the mission given.

All who are called will go through this challenge. Anyone denying it is only fooling him or herself. Prayers for one another are essential in overcoming failure. I shall always accept prayer from others since God's grace that gives me inner strength is found in these prayers. His kingdom is at work.

Jesus experienced overwhelming pressure. A study of the Gospels shows Jesus encountering crowds on numerous occasions. On one occasion, He disappeared for fear of being crushed by this crowd (Mark 3:7–12). Jesus was overwhelmed and felt the need to pray at a place called Gethsemane (Matthew 26:36). Aside from being overwhelmed by all the people with enormous needs, Jesus only had a few others willing to help Him. Jesus knows our struggles, and He will remain loyal to us as we continue His mission. God the Father promised this same loyalty in

Deuteronomy 31:6. Based on this promise, what is our mission in the kingdom of God?

THE MISSION

The people must first believe that God has called them.[39] I firmly believe God called me to serve as a chaplain, but what happens after retirement? I already know that the kingdom of God will always operate in my life, but I must now learn *where* God wants me to serve. You might find yourself alone as I do on occasion, but someone will always join you. God does test our faith and we must trust in His promises. You may also find yourself among many Christian workers involved in a greater task. This never means your task has less importance since God blesses all His workers. There are three stories that can give us some idea as to what God calls us to do.

1. A radio program called *All Things Considered* reported that a man and his wife decided to purchase computers for the public school system without funds to buy computers. The task outgrew their ability to ship to all the locations…until others joined this couple. More men and trucks came to their rescue. Today it might be possible that these schools have more equipment than the wealthy schools.
2. A young teenage boy discovered some homeless people who had no blankets or food to eat. He asked his father for help in developing a plan for the purchase and delivery of blankets and food for these homeless people. They began the project but never revealed the cost or the amount of time they spent doing this labor of love. They only told of how these people responded and the fact others had joined them in this cause.

3. I believe *60 Minutes* had the story about deformed and unwanted children living someplace in the former Soviet Union. You might recall the exact location. After the tragic story of these children was told, numerous American couples inquired how they might adopt them (a common act of love from Americans). There was even a follow-up story showing how well these adopted children were doing, along with some of the problems these couples had with the Russian government.

These stories only represent a fraction of the unselfish, loving things being accomplished for the glory of God. Jesus was correct when He said, "The harvest is plentiful, but the laborers are few." Jesus does send us out to a mission "as lambs in the midst of wolves" (Luke 10:2). His mission will not be easy, and the people in those three stories will tell you that. The seventy people whom Jesus sent out also experienced hardship.

Prayer for the Mission

The people must pray before entering the mission (Luke 10:5). It appears from this verse that Jesus asked us to pray before entering any mission. This request ultimately means that God is responsible. God is known to manipulate events, as He did between Moses and Pharaoh. He'll bless whom He chooses, as He did between Jacob and the angel. Prayers to God were offered first in these examples. We *must* pray before entering any mission—witnessing to other people, teaching a Sunday school lesson, entering a worship service or any other form of ministry. Prayer is the most effective means for a Spirit-led ministry.

The Mission Plan

The people must set up a well-organized plan (Luke 10:4, 7). Jesus had His own reason for telling the disciples to "carry no purse, no bag, no sandals; and salute no one on the road....Remain in the same house, eating and drinking what they provide, for the laborer deserves his wages." Perhaps one interpretation for this scripture could be recognizing the importance of having a well-organized plan. For example, one should *prioritize* the most important dates of the various goals that must be completed, prioritize sequential events, and develop purposes for each task in the mission. God will then bless a well-organized plan.

It is a privilege for us to have such a responsibility. Jesus apparently wants us to learn this lesson, but He also warns us that there is a cost for being committed to the plan (Luke 10:3).

A well-organized plan never tolerates comfort, complacency, self-satisfaction or personal gain (Luke 10:10). I noticed people with these traits become too blind to see their errors and too deaf to hear other people's disapproval of their plan. Jesus told His disciples, when they were not welcomed in certain towns, to wipe off the dust from their feet and move on.

Visit the Sick

A well-trained person must be selected to visit the sick (Luke 10:9). This particular mission is too important to send an unqualified person. Their illness can be very complicated and dangerous. I recall as an army hospital chaplain seeing a young dead soldier with his brain half outside of his skull. This is not the scene for an untrained person. Family members would be too distraught from such a scene.

Send a strong and well-seasoned person to offer spiritual comfort and support. A clinically trained chaplain has this skill. Jesus came into this world to heal the sick and forgive sins. He knows the challenge and will minister through His servants in this healing of the sick. He provides inner-strength and wisdom to His skillfully trained servants. I often sensed His grace overshadowing and comforting me during those rough days.

I recall ministering one day in four death situations. I finally had to walk outside to get some fresh air. There are numerous other stories I could tell, but these make my point. Jesus wants a well-trained servant to minister to the sick. The kingdom of God operates best in this kind of mission.

The King's Messenger

We must understand that this presentation will not be totally definitive. My purpose is only to encourage an interest in further study.

The King's Messenger is more popularly known as Jesus; however, we shall adapt the role of prophet / preacher as *messenger* for Christ. We shall also present this study in the Judaic context. Jesus came to the Jews first to deliver His gospel message, and He presented it in a language they understood. Yes, we will consider some Christian views about the King's messenger. We begin with God's contact with His people and how they were told to approach God.

No Fear

The messenger approached free from fear (Matthew 10:26–27). Jesus was clearly known by many as being very different from other men: He spoke with divine authority.

He apparently had a deep sense of concern for people to have a freedom from fear.

We have at least two reasons for having a freedom from fear: (a) There will always be someone or some event that will unveil the truth about unethical practices; and (b) Jesus commands us to proclaim boldly His message. Nothing could be farther from the truth. The truth will triumph. There is a Latin proverb that states: "Truth is great and truth will prevail."[40] At one moment of his life, James VI threatened to hang Andrew Melville for not telling something. Andrew's answer to James VI was, "You cannot hang or exile the truth." Church history also teaches that numerous early Christians had to suffer immensely for the cause of truth, which ultimately prevailed in spite of their suffering. These powerful people could not cover up or hide the truth from the world since there were other people, like Andrew Melville and the early Christians who were free from fear. What a paradox!

We should never be afraid to speak boldly God's message. Jesus commands us to proclaim Him: "What I tell you in the darkness, speak in the light. What you hear whispered in your ear, proclaim on the housetop" (Matthew 10:27).

Here lies the true function of the preacher / minister:

1. The preacher / minister must listen. No one can proclaim the truth unless they first listen to the truth. Erasmus wrote back to Colet at Oxford: "With what effrontery shall I teach what I have never learned? How am I to warm the coldest of others, when I am shivering myself?"[41]
2. The preacher / minister must speak what he or she has heard from Christ even if it gains him or her the hatred of

people or takes his / her life in his / her own hands. Someone said of John Knox, as they buried him, "Here lies one who feared God so much that he never feared the face of any man."[42] Many others have learned how to be free from fear.

COURAGE

The messenger approached with the right courage (Matthew 10:29–30). Jesus taught that there is *no* punishment that compares with the ultimate fate of a person who has been guilty of infidelity and disobedience to God. We therefore must note the three following things:

1. A belief in conditional immortality teaches that the reward of goodness is that the soul of a good person climbs up and up until he or she is one with all immortality—the bliss and the blessedness of God. Also, the punishment of the evil person, who will not mend his /her ways in spite of all of God's appeals to him or her, is a soul that goes down and down until it is finally obliterated, extinguished, annihilated and ceases to be.[43]
2. A Christian will acknowledge holy fear. We already mentioned that the Jews know all about holy fear. Their scholastic thinkers did not forget that there is love, and that love is the greatest of all things. These scholastic thinkers said: "Act from love, for there is no love where there is fear, or fear where there is love, except in relation to God."[44] In relation to God, there is always fear and love. Fear God and love God—the Law says both. If you hate, no lover hates; if you kick, no fearer kicks. As for Christians, our fear is not that God will punish us, but our fear is that we may grieve His love. God is love, but God is also holiness, for God is pure.

3. Disloyalty is worse than death. If one is guilty of disloyalty, he or she buys security at the expense of dishonor, life is no longer tolerable. One cannot face others, him or herself, and ultimately cannot face God. There is a time when comfort, safety, ease and life itself can cost too much.

God Cares

The messenger believes God does care. Why should we fear a God Who cares about us? We often hear it said: "If God cares enough for the sparrows, how much more will God care about His own people?" God will always care for all. The Jews have a thorough understanding of this argument. The rabbinical saying claims, "God sits and feeds the world, from the horns of the buffalo to the eggs of the louse."[45] God's love for His people is seen not only in the omnipotence of creation and in the great events of history, it is also seen in the day-to-day nourishment of the bodies of all people. The King's messenger knows that his / her time on earth is forever in God's hands; that God will not leave him or her; and that he or she is surrounded forever by the care of God. Of whom shall we be afraid?

Loyalty

The messenger approached with loyalty to Christ (Matthew 10:32–33). These verses bring a double loyalty to the Christian life. For example: If we are loyal to Christ while living on earth, then Jesus will be loyal to us in the life to come. Let us therefore be proud to acknowledge that Jesus is indeed Lord and Master, and he will also be proud to acknowledge us as being His servants. Pling, the Governor of Bithynia, wrote to the Roman emperor, Trajan, that all Christians would not worship anyone but the name of Jesus, nor would Pling be able to shake their loyalty.

Perhaps we should consider three ways a person can deny Christ and still claim to believe in him.

1. **We deny Christ with our words**. J. P. Mahaffy, the famous scholar and man of the world from Trinity College, Dublin, once answered "Yes" to whether or not he was indeed a Christian; but his Christianity did not interfere with the society he kept and the pleasures he loved.[46] Mr. Mahaffy wanted to escape his duty of being different from the world. This action is one way to deny Christ.

2. **We deny Christ by our silence.** A French story was told that a French writer brought his young wife into an old family that did not approve of their marriage. The writer's family was also too polite for verbal objection. His wife, afterwards, said her whole married life was a misery by the menace of things unsaid. We must utter words of protest against evil to take a stand and show which side we are on. Silence is another form of denial of Christ.[47]

3. **We deny Christ by our actions.** We can live a life that completely denies the faith in which we profess. We who gave allegiance to the gospel and are still guilty—of petty dishonesties, breaches of strict honor, living a dominate life of ease and comfort, being bitter and resentful with various people—most assuredly would bring into question whether the idea of Christian service, charity and generosity are indeed conspicuous by their absence in a faith. Perhaps this prayer composed for the Lambeth Conference of 1948 will give us proper guidance: "Almighty God, give us grace to be not only hearers, but doers of Thy Holy Word, not only to admire, but to obey Thy doctrine, not only to profess, but to practice Thy religion, not only to love, but to live

Thy Gospel. So grant that what we learn of Thy glory we may receive into our hearts, and show forth in lives: through Jesus Christ our Lord. Amen."[48] A life lived like this prayer would indeed represent loyalty by the King's messenger and a reward in itself.

The Cost

The messenger approached knowing the cost. Jesus offers the cross as the cost for being loyal to Him. People in His day knew very well what the cross means. The Roman general, Varus, broke the revolt of Judas of Galilee when he crucified 2,000 Jews and placed the crosses along the roads of Galilee for people to see. In ancient days the criminal actually carried the crossbeam, as Jesus carried it, to the place of crucifixion. Some people even staggered and died in agony before the crucifixion. Christians may be required to sacrifice personal desires and dreams for the purpose of doing Christ's will. They only need to be ready and willing.

Christ offered people an adventure: The one who finds his/her life will lose it, and those who lose his/her life for His namesake will find it. Any Christian who takes a stand for Christ most likely makes a difference between what society now has and what they would have lost. There is no place for security and no cost in Christianity.

The Reward

The messenger approached knowing the reward. Jesus made Himself very clear when He said those who receive you also receive Him; and they who receive Him also receive Him Who sent Jesus. The Jews understood this concept. Anyone who receives an ambassador pays respect to the king who sent that ambassador. Honoring the ambassador is to honor his king. The rabbis say, "He who shows hospitality to the wise is as if he brought the firstfruits of his produce unto God. He who greets the learned is as if he greeted God."[49] If one is true to God, he or she shall receive all people just as though he or she receives God Himself. Who among us can treat a homeless beggar with such reverence? We should therefore see four links in this teaching:

1. God Who offers salvation.
2. Jesus Who brought the message.
3. The messenger / prophet who spoke.
4. The believers who received the messenger.

Let us be mindful that those who give hospitality to the messenger will receive no less a reward than the messenger himself. Those who have thankless jobs of making a home, cooking meals, washing clothes, shopping for household necessities, caring for children and who never think of it as a dreary job, will more likely receive the messenger's reward than those people whose days are filled with committees.

The Cobbler

H.L. Gee once told a story of a cobbler who never became a minister. The cobbler never had the opportunity to receive the appropriate education. His pastor once came to his place of business to have some shoes repaired. The cobbler gave his pastor a pair of new shoes with the understanding that these shoes would be worn during the worship service. The cobbler was preaching the gospel and *not* the pastor. There was no greater reward for the cobbler than welcoming the King's messenger.

We learned the awesome responsibility that comes from being The King's messenger. We also learned that the messenger is actually living proof of how the kingdom of God works.

The Kingdom in a Divided Church

The most difficult thing to comprehend is that God's kingdom was fulfilled in a divided church.[50] Impossible? No, Christ's church can be divided in a fulfilled kingdom of God. The point is that God's action remains actively fulfilled even while His people cause divisions among themselves. I came to this conclusion after considering both themes in the Gospel of Matthew (4:12–23) and Paul's letter to Corinth (1 Corinthians 1:10–17). Isaiah 9:1–4 gives us a chance to rejoice when God's people see the light of God's mercy and love for them. Isaiah also prophesied Jesus as the Light that the people finally saw, even until this day. Matthew 4:16: "The people who sat in darkness have seen a great light, and for those who sat in the region and shadow of death, light has dawned."

God always offers a salvation of soul, body and mind to His people who also have the right to accept or reject it. God's plan and work always continue while His people always confront one another. These two worlds operate on separate energies, and they seldom reflect exact and precise similarities. Let us therefore look at these two worlds to learn how they coexist separately.

Life and Death

The kingdom rules over life and death in a divided church. God cares how the suffering people endure from such diseases as cancer. His kingdom rules over such suffering and gives peace—inner-strength of the soul, body and mind—and gives grace to learn how to live before dying. When Jesus spoke about life and death, He always looked beyond the physical body where one can find a spiritual life and death. Jesus' words from John 8:51: "If anyone keeps my word, he or she will never see death." By interpretation *death* is actually *sin*, and Jesus promised that we actually will not see sin if we follow Him as our Lord and Savior. Although Jesus looks more at our spiritual life, His kingdom still rules over our suffering.

In the midst of suffering the church became divided over such issue as intellectualized Christianity. The Apostle Paul wrote about this issue to the people at Corinth when he mentioned Appolos, a Jew from Alexandria. It appeared to Paul that Appolos and his followers were turning Christianity into a philosophical religion. He turned Christianity into a science by allegorizing the Scriptures and finding endless amount of meaning from the simplest verse. The average Christian could not deal with this person, and his efforts began to divide Christ's church. The Apostle Paul had to bring about a healing for the church. As this happened, God's kingdom still ruled and was fulfilled.

Eternal Life

The kingdom brought eternal life to Israel in a divided church. The Israelites never discussed eternal life until the concept of resurrection began to be debated. Previous to this debate, people only knew about such concepts as living a long life, experiencing family blessings, having prosperity and fellowshipping with God. Not everyone believed in this new concept of *resurrection*. God's kingdom, at this time in history, was at work introducing a new mystery of God. Jesus nurtured this concept by extending God's kingdom to eternal life. The Israelites dealt only with the present age, but Jesus wanted to introduce God's people to eternal life. God's inclusion of eternal life in His kingdom was fulfilled, but not without divisions among Israel. Hence, the followers of Jesus began to form another group known as Christ's *church*.[51]

The tension between these two groups, the people of Israel and Christ's church, began to surface again. Paul also mentioned Cephas in his letter to Corinth. Cephas had followers who taught Christians must continue with the Jewish Law. They exalted the Law and belittled grace. Cephas also taught that Jesus only belonged to them (the exclusion of Gentiles). Paul's mission was to unite these people who were divided. God's kingdom continued to rule even during this tragic conflict.

Present Day

The kingdom rules during our age as well by offering an abundant life and eternal life. We are assured of this eternal life from the resurrection of Lazarus. The voice of Jesus can be heard and obeyed by the dead. His authority over life and death should convince us that Jesus is able to offer protection, wisdom, social and spiritual guidance, peace and hope. Jesus not only lived among the people 2,000 years ago, but He continues to live among us today. He also continues to reveal some knowledge about His Father to us through the Holy Spirit. The kingdom of God rules, indeed, during our age of a divided church.

The church in the 1990s is divided over a number of issues. There is disagreement over theology, doctrine and worship practices. We even have groups saying that Jesus only accepts them. Most of what I have already mentioned concerning the early Christian church seems to apply to the church of the nineties. This division is unfortunate, but thank God His kingdom continues to be fulfilled in a divided church.

Addendum Three

A Theology on Christian Faith

Christians come from an enriched culture and faith. The very moment they receive their faith from God, a development and enriched refinement of their faith begins (Luke 8:22–25). So it was during the transition between Jesus' ministry of three years and the apostolic ministry in Christ's church. Faith itself may well mean faithfulness (trustworthiness) in God's manifestations of grace in Israel's history; but it now reaches out to and lays hold of the saving act in Christ (Acts 4:12). A Christian's obedience in faith no longer trusts in the Ten Commandments, but rather, in the way of salvation of Christ.[52] There is confidence in Christ as well as His Father. There is the confidence that if we are dead in Christ, we shall also live with Him eternally.[53] Faith rhetorically expresses the beginning and ending of human life.

The human life of Jesus on earth had a physical beginning and ending. We mortals also share in these same physical experiences. Where should we differ from Jesus? We certainly differ by not being an immortal God. The mortal flesh of Jesus on earth obviously died on the cross and yet resurrected (John 20:1–23); but the immortal God in Jesus never died—and lives eternally. We cannot be any more different than this. We therefore need no other reason for believing, trusting, reaching out to and holding on to this gospel message of salvation. This rhetorical expression of faith by each Christian is uniquely different from others.

Fr. Daniel Berringan (S.T.) was uniquely different by being arrested on August 1970 for his antiwar activities. He was sentenced for three years in prison at Danbury, Connecticut. He was a theologian, teacher and a well-known poet. His only desire was to help other people to form a friendly unity. He was quoted as saying, "I die daily," for what apparently became his expression of faith. What is our expression of faith, and can it be expressed in a literary style so as to influence or persuade others? Let us explore faith in the context of rhetorical expressions.

Faith through Corporate Fellowship

A study of Mark 11:1–33 clearly defines how faith can be expressed through a corporate fellowship. In fact, one can easily prepare an order of service for a worship service from this scripture. I personally hope all worship services achieve this as a goal. We shall approach the question: "How is faith expressed through corporate fellowship?" with the following order of service format.

Opening Processional

Jesus triumphantly entered into Jerusalem on a colt as King of all kings and people shouting: "Hosanna! Blessed is the One Who comes in the name of the Lord! Blessed is the coming kingdom of our ancestor David! Hosanna in the highest heaven" (Mark 11:9–10). Surely, there is no greater opening for the processional than this. Each worship service ought to begin with such grandeur of persuasion that God is with us. Most Christian churches will conduct an elaborate opening processional on Palm Sunday or Easter; our Lord deserves this level of reverence weekly or for all worship service.

A Call to Worship

God calls all His people to worship Him in spirit and truth (John 4:23–24). We enter this corporate fellowship under the guidance and persuasion of the Holy Spirit along with being merely our own person. We also enter into this worship service reaching out to and holding on to Christ's promise of peace, hope, mercy and salvation. We finally enter into this worship service believing in God Almighty and that His Son, Christ Jesus, spoke only the truth. Our Lord acknowledges worship with His blessing and His challenge to bear fruit (Mark 11:14). This line of discussion somewhat reflects the Godhead/Trinity image.

There is indeed a fellowship within the Godhead / Trinity.[54] The Son of God and the Holy Spirit are under subjection to the supreme Almighty God, the Father. It is their mutual fellowship that symbolically reflects an image of corporate fellowship. We are created in His image (Genesis 1:26). We therefore should enjoy the same spiritual fellowship with one another.

Prayers of Confession and Repentance

All Christians are sinners (Luke 18:13). Our Lord favorably accepts our humble faith and attitude during the worship service just as He did with the tax collector. Mark 11:15–20 offers a strong message about His house being used only for prayer. It is a time to cleanse our soul from all unrighteous deeds. Our prayers of confession and repentance will indeed achieve this goal. Let us never enter a worship service without the desire to confess and repent of our sins.

God's Forgiveness and Pardon of Sins

Jesus has the authority to forgive sin (Matthew 9:6), and we have no right to question His authority (Mark 11:33). We should therefore enter into a worship service reaching out to and holding on to this promise that our sins will be forgiven and pardoned. Our celebration of this cleansing of the soul can be in the Holy Communion. We shall afterwards depart from one another in peace and with hope.

Corporate fellowship is now complete. Amen.

Faith Expressed through Spiritual Eyes

We just completed looking at a scripture that provides an outline for an order of service (Mark 11). This service could be quite fitting for the blind man, Bartimaeus, son of Timaeus (Mark 10:46–52). Jesus gave him eyesight, and he should have celebrated by worshipping God in accordance with the previous format. How did Bartimaeus gain a more favorable insight of Jesus' authority than the Jewish leadership? Most people with eyesight can see sincerity in a person's eye and body language. Bartimaeus could not enjoy this privilege, but, instead, he innately knew Jesus could give him his eyesight. Jesus claimed Bartimaeus's faith made him well. Bartimaeus' blindness did not prevent him from getting acquainted with Jesus. The Jewish leadership could have easily learned a lesson from Bartimaeus. Let us now step into the Jewish leadership's "sandals" for a moment to test whether or not they could have learned more from spiritual eyes.

The Holy Spirit

The Holy Spirit can be our spiritual eyes. A blind person with a guide dog is a very common practice in the twentieth century. I, frankly, cannot explain how a blind person can function today with a dog's guidance, due to my own ignorance. These dogs are an enormous blessing, and I also cannot think of one sufficient gift of appreciation that would be appropriate for them. Having said that about these dogs, and with a great amount of reverence, I want to claim that the Holy Spirit offers far more guidance for a blind person than what these incredible dogs are able to do.

The Holy Spirit enlightens us of the necessary facts about Jesus.

- He teaches us not to sin against Him (Mark 3:22–30).
- He was an active agent in the miraculous conception of Jesus (Luke 1:34 f.; Matthew 1:18).
- He was given by the Father, via the anointment of Jesus, to do good and to heal all who were oppressed by the devil (Acts 10:38).
- He is the Agent Who effects spiritual rebirth for us to enter the kingdom of Heaven (John 3:2 ff.).
- The important factor in Christian baptism is not water, but the Holy Spirit (John 3:8).

- He is our Advocate and represents truth (John 14:15–17).
- He is the Spirit of Christ (Romans 8:9, 14 ff.; 1 Corinthians 6:17; 2 Corinthians 3:17; Galatians 4:6).
- He guides the church (Acts 10:19, 44).

There are many more examples of the Holy Spirit's functions. These examples are also good for the welfare of the blind man, Bartimaeus.

Divine Testimonies

Bartimaeus most likely heard divine testimonies from Jesus and others. We can safely assume that Bartimaeus already believed in the God of Israel. His keen ears and mind most likely enabled him to learn and remember all the divine testimonies from Jesus' teachings and from others who taught. The blind man fully knew God could not lie (Titus 1:2), and for this reason, Bartimaeus believed in these testimonies. He finally "listened" to his spiritual heart, which was a channel for the Holy Spirit to communicate.

Spiritual Heart

Bartimaeus most likely listened to his spiritual heart. All the testimonies from Jesus and perhaps His disciples had a very positive impact on Bartimaeus's heart. He was convicted, as Christians say (James 2:9). Bartimaeus began at this point to reach out to and hold on to Christ's promises of peace, mercy and divine powers of healing. With such a background, who could be surprised at Bartimaeus's strong faith that Jesus could give eyesight? Unfortunately, the Jewish leadership was not only surprised, but also offended. Bartimaeus's experiences are substantive examples of spiritual eyes in one's faith.

Faith through Humility, Persistence and Unconditional Trust

Jesus was apparently very tired after His difficult debate with the political leaders of Jerusalem (Matthew 15:1–20), and decided to move northwestern from Gennesaret to the eastern border of Phoenicia. It was here that he heard the Canaanite woman shouting, "Have mercy on me, Lord, Son of David; my daughter is tormented by demons" (Matthew 15:22). There was an obvious pause before Jesus and this woman had a discussion. Her Gentile background was an uncomfortable situation for the Jews, and Jesus knew this. His response to her was to explain that His mission should be to Jews first. But she replied, "Yes, Lord, yet even the dogs eat the crumbs that fall from their masters' table" (Matthew 15:27). This woman now had Jesus' attention.

Jesus apparently recognized such qualities as humility, persistence and unconditional trust in the Canaanite woman's faith (Matthew 15:21–28). Jesus also wanted to make this an issue since very few people had these qualities in their faith. Consequently, the Canaanite woman's special faith was not only the reason for her daughter's healing, but also these qualities of faith are absolutely essential for learning. They even rank higher than learning the Law of Moses. Jesus knew these laws did not focus on such qualities of faith. We therefore should not be surprised at such a lack of knowledge by the house of Israel. Let us now consider these three qualities of faith.

HUMILITY

Humility should be in our faith. By definition we can easily say this woman showed humility. She was not self-assertive, proud or lacking self-respect. She only knew her daughter deserved divine healing and was willing to confront Jesus by humbling herself. She even accepted herself as being equal with dogs, but insisted on receiving the crumbs from the table that the dogs get. This apparently impressed Jesus and clearly gave Him a way to teach the lesson on humility we need to learn.

Jesus taught respect and recognition of the poor and lowly during His transaction with the Canaanite woman (Matthew 15:28; Mark 7:29–30). Jesus taught that our faith ought to include humility like that woman's humility. The people of Israel might well have been God's first choice, but that should never put any greater importance on Israel than other people.

Let us consider a comparative example: One person can be first in a particular line while all the others are in the same line with equal access to whatever is being given. Just as one person is first in line, there shall also be only one winner. That person in either case should never have the reputation of being better than others. God's blessings will never run out, but perhaps waiting for our turn in line will strengthen our faith in the process. The woman knew this lesson better than the disciples did. She also knew persistence.

Persistence

Persistence should be in our faith. How should the Canaanite woman's persistence be defined? Was she stubborn, enduring continuance with a chosen course or purpose? Did she have a strong tenacity or a simple vision? We can only speculate, but the language in both Matthew and Mark clearly shows the woman refusing to relent, especially in face of opposition by Jesus' comment about the dog. I have this same kind of stubbornness and can identify with this woman. I am triggered by such demeaning word as dog. I learned from this passage of Scripture that stubbornness can be positive. I can be stubborn toward a positive end. The Canaanite woman had this quality of faith that brought about a positive result for her daughter's recovery. The demons were removed.

The Canaanite woman did not have a vision or any knowledge of Moses' Law. She was a mother with very strong tenacity. She had to be tough in order to survive. Her world was not a pleasant place to live. A mother's instinct of her children's welfare will always be spontaneous and compelling enough to get results. She obviously possessed a persistent quality of faith. She had another quality as well.

Unconditional Faith

We should have unconditional faith. God wants us to trust in Him without any conditions attached. He loves us without any conditions attached, and we should not have hidden agendas while expressing gratitude. The woman had unconditional trust in Jesus, that He would indeed heal her daughter. She only had that one pure expectation and no conditions for it. She asked nothing for herself except the fulfillment of her God-given love for her daughter. Perhaps we can say the woman placed her faith under the Messianic Lordship of Christ, and, for this reason, He granted her request.

Would all the twentieth-century mothers do the very same thing for their children? The answer would be a judgment call since I know some mothers who have been overpowered by substance abuses and have utterly failed their children. But I am confident that a great majority of mothers are very much like the Canaanite woman. These mothers want everything for their children and nothing for themselves. They would indeed sacrifice their own lives for the protection of their own children, and most likely others as well. This is unconditional love.

The latest tragedy for these mothers is having an adult child with AIDS. I personally cannot recall one mother rejecting her adult child with AIDS. I met a father who did, however. My first hospital ministry with AIDS patients was in mid 1984, and they continued until my retirement on June 1, 1994. These mothers never privately confessed their disappointment but, rather, gave continuous support. These mothers had unconditional love for their children who died from AIDS. All the moments exchanged between these mothers and their adult children never ended without tears.

One can surely imagine the tears between the Canaanite woman and her daughter. We also can imagine the feelings that Jesus had for them. Her strong faith epitomized what faith ought to be. Her actions and responses to Jesus could be characterized as being similar to the struggles between Jacob and the angel at Jabbok River (Genesis 32:22–32).

Rear-Line Faith

A soldier fighting on the front line witnessed the horrors of war. The imagery was fused in the mind and consequently caused the contemporary diagnose of Post-Traumatic Stress Disorder (PTSD). Any familiar sound or image can triggers a very frightening response in that former combat veteran. Did this veteran have faith in his God while fighting on the front line? The immediate answer is yes, but I chose to offer it in the context of what I call the rear-line thoughts.

There is only one thought a soldier has when confronting the enemy on the front line: "I hope like hell I get out of this alive." A soldier will experience confusion, anger, resentment and fear during this confrontation. One might intellectually perceive a sense of rear-line thinking concerning one's faith during any given combat situation. However, any expression of that faith will only surface when there is still a hope of remaining alive. All other thoughts, such as confusion, anger, resentment and fear, will clearly motivate a soldier to make good and bad decisions.

One soldier told me about a moment he could never get out of his mind. He was fighting in the deep jungles of Vietnam, when suddenly he and his enemy were face to face with jammed weapons; they could not fire. He thought 30 seconds passed before they both decided to walk off in opposite directions. Those few seconds felt much longer, and all the energy he had was absolutely gone. Both soldiers were obviously horrified over that experience. The American soldier's hope to remain alive certainly affirmed his personal faith. His rear-line thinking about faith suddenly went to the front line of his mind.

An easier way to explain a soldier's faith is simply this: A soldier has as much thought about faith as the average person on the street. They exist in the subconscious mind and will not rush to the fore until a sudden, horrifying experience occurs. Although the soldiers from America and Vietnam have personal faith, we should consider three acceptable concepts that have a positive impact on one's faith.

1. We should know about Almighty God's Fatherhood. We can find the concept of God's "Fatherhood" in Galatians 1:3–10. It is not adequate to define the concept in terms of a human fatherhood, but rather express it in the sense of Almighty Father versus believers. His "Fatherhood" profoundly mandates that the sins of believers be removed via the death of God's Son, Christ Jesus. This same Almighty God, through Christ, chose the Apostle Paul to be His ambassador and to preach the gospel message (Galatians 1:16). Unfortunately, Paul had anonymous "co-workers," perhaps the Judaizers in the churches of Galatia, who decided to confuse the believers (1:6–9). Paul had to change the believers' minds since he knew his accusers were wrong (1:8). The Heavenly Father only wants the very best from all believers (5:22–26). Is it not equally unfortunate that some twentieth-century Christians became the same believers that Paul's accusers were?

God's Fatherhood expects all believers to become upright, impeccable examples for the world to witness. He expects all human fathers to love their own children by living a life worthy of God's praise. He expects husbands and wives to remain faithful to each other; children to respect their elders; neighbors to love one another as He loves them. He expects the church leadership to teach the truth, to feed the poor and provide shelter for the homeless. God expects all believers to seek His righteousness through His Son, Christ Jesus (Galatians 3:11; 5:16–21). These are high expectations from God but they come from His love. The Apostle Paul strongly appealed to all the believers in Galatia to accept God's love and His Fatherhood.[55] We can do nothing less.

2. **We should know the Savior and Christ.** We begin with Jesus in the human race and having a history in our world. Most books would say this man, Who later became identified as God's Son and Who had prior existence with the

Father in heaven, had a primary mission to give Himself for our sins (Romans 8:3, 1 Corinthians 15:3). He was anointed as Christ, the Savior for all believers.[56] The problem tends to lie in the acceptance.

Many people take a whole lifetime to accept Jesus as the Christ and Savior of the world. Perhaps the biblical person, (doubting) Thomas, represents them. I once had a patient who finally accepted Christ as his Savior at the age of 65. He had less than one year to fulfill God's expectations before he died. His wife told me about his smile at death. I cannot think of a better way to die.

3. **We should know about God's unlimited divine power (Luke 6:6–11, 17–19; 7:1–17).** People today are much less likely to acknowledge a healing of the body since so many false, self-claimed divine healers exist. Numerous medical professionals also share those doubts. None the less, Jesus conducted unlimited divine healing. He restored a man's withered hand, healed diseases, healed unclean spirits, and He raised a dead man. These are spectacular events, but they are also unexplainable. It requires faith in God's words to believe in these events as being true. They become God's way of demonstrating His power. He did this all through His redemptive history, and this will continue until the completion of God's kingdom. God indeed has power over the living and the dead.

A combat soldier can easily store all of these memorable healing events in the back of his / her mind and still go into a combat situation. The scriptures about God's unlimited divine power offers hope for this soldier to get out of the "hell" one experiences in war. There is no end to God's power of healing, protection, or instilling inner-strength and confidence against the enemy. A soldier who knows and believes in God's Fatherhood, Christ as the Savior and God's unlimited divine power to uplift faith will have a positive impact. One's faith is indeed increased by such an impact.

Five Ways to Keep the Faith

We often exhort one another to "keep the faith." What ever do we mean by this exhortation? At a very serious moment when someone is suffering the loss of a loved one, we lovingly and softly say, "Keep the faith." Christians say to one another, when going their separate ways, "Keep the faith." Pastors exhort their parishioners at the conclusion of a worship service to "keep the faith." But again, what do we mean?

We all live in hopes of a peaceful and meaningful life. We also know life includes both positive and negative elements. We are taught that faith offers us the one and only answer to life's problems. These add up to one conclusion: We must keep the faith. Let us consider five ways to do so.

Keep the Commandments

We are told to serve God with all our heart and soul and to keep His commandments and statutes (Deuteronomy 10:12–13). I suggest that our heart is symbolic of the life we now have—a life that includes breathing and having a healthy body. Our soul is symbolic of the spiritual life we enjoy—life with fellow Christians at church. Keeping His commandments and statutes help us to accomplish all this.

I knew people who only chose to acknowledge the need to honor his / her heart. Without it they could not live, and they realized this. For them, their heart is necessary for living and accomplishing whatever they desire; they place no other importance on it. They alone accomplish their goals and not God's. These people serve no one else but their employer and themselves. As for their soul, they seldom say much beyond the fact that it may exist. They also claim that there is no life after death. They consider their body as simply an empty object after death. These people keep their faith only in themselves.

Other people, who search for more than the acknowledgment of just the biological need for their heart, will consider their soul to have a special purpose. They sense a greater power beyond themselves. They will accept a spiritual purpose for their heart and soul. After this acceptance, they believe in God Almighty, and they look to sources where their faith can absorb spiritual maturity. They look in God's Word—the Bible. It instructs them on how to live with faith in God, and how to accept His only Son as their Lord of life. They learn that, without a belief in Christ Jesus, there is no life; just as there is no life without a heart. Life requires more than just a heart; life requires both a heart and soul. One's faith is kept alive by maintaining a search for spiritual maturity. This search is one reason we say to keep the faith; it is essential for our heart.

Fear God

We are told to cleave to God through fear (Deuteronomy 10:12, 20). We shall keep our faith as long as we fear god. Some may ask, "Why should we fear God Who loves us?" Theologically, this notion began with God's initial fellowship with Abraham and his descendants. The relationship was compared to a father and his children.[57] A father always loves his children enough to discipline them. Children learn to fear the discipline and not the love from their father. God's children have the same kind of love relationship. Keith Miller identified the tough love concept in his earliest books. He claimed a father should never jeopardize his love for a child by very strong disciplinary actions of a child's poor behavior.

I once saw on the news media a few teenagers that destroyed homes, which caused about $150,000.00 damages. Their parents had a very serious disciplinary problem to face, along with an enormous debt. A few states have begun to hold all parents responsible for their children's criminal actions. Keith Miller would advise these parents to show tough love, which hopefully gets them through that incredible situation. Even with this in mind, God still offers hope. The good news is the fact that results from harsh judgments will indeed mold a person into a mature individual. These teenagers will most likely criticize their parents, but they will eventually change to respect their parents. A parent never compromises appropriate discipline to just be "accepted" by their children. The best gift parents can give their children is the knowledge and understanding of being responsible for any action. Grace and mercy are given only to the repentant person. God shows us the same tough love, and our response is usually to show respect and reverence. It is also our second way we keep the faith.

Swear by God's Name

We are told to swear by His name, for all He did (Deuteronomy 10:20–21). Christians tend to use the name of Jesus, or Christ, after prayer. There is no difference in this situation than what Deuteronomy commands since Jesus is in the Godhead; He is both man and God. The primary reason is surrendering our obedience and gratitude toward God's goodness. This action is keeping loyal to our faith.

A brief review of our lives will demonstrate the different examples of the use of God's name. Prayer was already mentioned. This can be done during worship services or at any place we might inhabit. Making important decisions can be another opportunity—entering a career or purchasing a home. There is a sense of partnership with God and a feeling of protection when we submit a decision to Him. People find peace of mind and hope for the future when this action is taken. An oath taken during a court trial is still another example. We are told to say, "I swear that this testimony that I am about to give is true, so help me, God." We shall be legally responsible for any statement we make, and only the truth shall be told. This action is also a testimony of our faith. It shows that we are not willing to mock the name of God, but we are keeping the faith.

Finish the Race

We are told to finish the race of life (2 Timothy 4:7). Pastors often use this text for a sermon, and it can become very lengthy and definitive. The Apostle Paul's life serves as a great example for how faith was kept alive. He indeed suffered many criticisms, endured many tortures and achieved many accomplishments for Christ's church. He did all this at the risk of his health as well. Paul called it a good fight to finish the race and keep the faith.

You and I are in this same race of life. We are criticized, exploited, robbed, beaten, killed and much more. Today's race is tough, and it requires a strong and lasting faith. Aside from a need for God's grace and mercy, we also need each other. Let's keep our faith alive as we endure our good fight and finish the race of life. To God be the glory; we are blessed. Amen.

Humble Yourself

We are finally told to humble ourselves in prayer. The easiest way to explain this is to do the opposite of the Pharisees' prayers. Their prayers are an effrontery to God's holiness and reverence. This action truly separates one from God's fellowship and a loss of faith. The Pharisees could have learned humility from a tax collector (Luke 18:9–14). The tax collector prayed, "God, be merciful to me, a sinner!"

Prayers with temerity toward God have no future fellowship. Only a person with pure humility from the very depths of their heart and soul could understand. Some people reach this understanding at an early date in life, but others tend to take longer. Perhaps the well-known parable of the prodigal son would be an example of the earlier date (Luke 15:11–24). This son learned that even his father's hired hands had a better life than his. He decided to ask his father to accept him as one of the hired hands. He showed humility before his father and not a shameless attitude. His father had compassion and welcomed him joyfully. This story should serve as a way of explaining how one needs to approach God prayerfully.

An elderly, dying patient of mine had a lifetime battle with God. This was at least his wife's story. She came to me in tears, begging me to talk with her husband about salvation. I learned this was her desire and not the patient's. Both of us went to the patient's bedside, and I simply began with small talk. He was most likely aware that his wife had asked for support in her concern. The patient eventually asked if I would explain about salvation in light of his wife's concern. I asked if this is what he wanted, and he said yes. Our discussion was lengthy, and there were times when the patient could not understand some of my explanations. I decided this was due to politeness. I then asked him if I could be cold and factual. He agreed and soon he understood. He claimed that he had never heard such a clear message about salvation. He and his wife were in tears as he asked me to pray for him. He humbled himself in prayer. This patient spent his life fighting with God. Each person is responsible for his/her own humility and keeping the faith.

Lack of Faith and a Need for Confession

We live in a very complex, highly judgmental society. Christians are being critically judged for their superficial faith and how they live. I recall a medical doctor saying to me that Christians even appear to fear death more than non-Christians do. I personally observe a serious lack of understanding about simple messages in the Bible. Therefore, I make it my business to teach those truths in my sermons because of that observation.

How Faith is Expressed

There is a striking similarity between two healings that shows how faith is expressed (Mark 7:31–37; 8:22–30). Jesus had great compassion and a sensitivity to the need for privacy of these two men who were healed. He took them away from a crowd of people and then used techniques of patient care, known only by the people of that century and culture. Jesus was fully aware that these men had serious limitations: one could not hear or tell a person what he understood, and the other could not totally see people or objects. The use of spit was a common clinical practice by physicians of that century, along with magic shows. These men were not surprised. Many doctors today could learn a lesson on bedside manor from our Lord. Jesus realized that these men would feel more at ease being treated on a one-to-one basis. He looked to the heavens so they would know God was with them.

I often had opportunities to observe students and intern doctors treating patients. Whenever I noticed how they could improve the doctor-and-patient relationship, I would convince these doctors to take my advice. I obviously did the same for my own clinical, pastoral, educational students as well. A patient needs to trust and respect his/her doctor and chaplain. A doctor can never get that trust and respect by using such medical terms as Chronic Obstructive Pulmonary Disease or Multiple Infarct Dementia, or by touching someone's body without any previous explanation about the purpose for the exam. Another prevention of trust and respect was on the local news about a surgeon amputating the wrong foot. This kind of tragic failure requires an enormous amount of explanation. It is easily avoidable if the doctor would have maintained proper precautions.

Chaplains are equally responsible for the prevention of offensive comments and the abuse of privileged communications. Such irresponsible pastoral care will never gain trust and respect. Jesus knew all this quite well and demonstrated how one should treat patients. He knew these two men would be too frightened in a crowd. He also knew these men would not understand what Jesus was doing unless he took the time privately to instruct and treat them in separate stages, as they were accustomed.

Jesus asked the blind man, "Do you see anything?"

And his reply was, "I see men; but they look like trees walking."

Jesus again laid His hands upon the man's eyes; now the man saw everything clearly. Jesus was still concerned,

"Do not even enter the village." The impact of seeing a crowd of people would be too great for a man who had recently been blind. Jesus felt the blind man had to gradually become accustomed to seeing his immediate environment before he tried seeing many other exciting things and people. Most scholars agree with this explanation of Jesus' reasons for conducting the healing as He had done; but there is another explanation, which borders more on the negative approach.

A few scholars claim Jesus had demonic associations to consider. His approach to healing could very well have been associated with Gentile demonic practices. People in the villages would quickly make this association, and therefore Jesus had to guard against it. This precaution would explain why He went out of the village and privately treated those men, and why Jesus asked those men not to enter the village. The healing was also conducted on Gentile soil. I find this explanation rather limits Jesus and His divine authority. There wasn't any demonic influence.

Hearing God

Faith can be expressed through hearing God. Jesus apparently had some concerns for people not hearing His divine message (Mark 4:3–24; 6:7; 8:18). Even His disciples were "deaf and blind to the word of God" (Mark 8:18; 9:7). People could not explain their faith, and they were, therefore, too vulnerable to poor theological teachings. I have been wondering why God's church today still has the same symptoms. We have God's Word to instruct us and provide a foundation for our faith. The church leadership is responsible for offering this instruction and foundation. I consider any hospital as an appropriate testing ground for the instructions of church leadership.

There are patients in these hospitals who need prayer for every small matter that comes up during treatment; they never consider praying for themselves. They cannot explain the essence of the four Gospels or the Book of Acts. They do not have a clear understanding of the various versions of the Bible. They have little knowledge of Jesus' parables. Something must be done.

The church leadership of these patients must begin training their "children," offering a strong theological foundation. There must be strong teaching programs for all ages. A weak congregation needs a consultant to come in to assess their whole educational program. There must be a change so no one is deaf and blind to the Word of God. We must listen to hear God.

Confession

Faith is especially expressed by confession. A brief look at John 9:9–11 will allow us to imagine the blind man shouting with happiness: "The man called Jesus made clay, anointed my eyes and said to me, 'Go to Siloan and wash.' So I went and washed and received my sight." God's work was affirmed in this blind man; a great reason to shout with praise and thanksgiving, and a great confession that Jesus is the Christ. Praise be to God. Amen.

Let us go back to the Gospel of Mark 8:27–30 to reflect on another confession. Scholars agree that this portion of Scripture was inserted as a theological message on true confession. Jesus asked His disciples, "Who do men say that I am?"

Their first two answers were "John the Baptist" and "Elijah."

And then Jesus asked again, "But who do you say that I am?"

Peter's answer was, "You are the Christ." His answer to Jesus was not only a message to the world—that Jesus is the Christ with divine authority over life and death—but it was to be internalized within our souls. This is indeed a true confession.

Can we confess Jesus as being the Christ with divine authority? Can we refer back in our lives to a moment similar to what these two men had? I am certain we can. Our moment with Jesus does not need the same experience. Ours will be unique to us personally. Jesus will approach you privately and treat your spiritual or physical illness according to your own understanding. He will treat you in stages, never to cause you any fear, but offering the greatest respect and love for your needs. Let us therefore exercise our own true faith and truly confess that Jesus is the Christ and Lord of lords. Praise be to God. Amen.

Conclusion

We learned there are at least six ways to express our faith. The most common thread we find in all six is by reaching out to and laying hold of the saving act of Christ (Acts 4:12). We now can live with confidence that if we die in Christ, we shall also live with Him eternally.[58] Amen.

Addendum Four

A Theology on Divine Love

The word love in the English language has its limitations. There is the usage of strong affection for attachment, or devotion to a person or persons; a strong liking or interest in something: as, her love for acting; a strong, usually passionate, affection for a person of the opposite sex. And finally, the person who is the object of such affection: a sweetheart / lover. Now we can review a theological understanding of God's Love.

In theology, the word is used in the sense of God's benevolent concern for His people; His people's devout attachment to God. Love under the Hebrew or Greek context can be summed up by an earnest and anxious desire for, and an active and beneficent interest in, the well being of the one loved. This study will attempt to offer a definitive theological and biblical understanding of God's Love.

The Vertical Love Relationship

We begin with a love relationship between God and His people. Often the supernatural nature of the Godhead is clearly demonstrated in this relationship by showing God's substantive love for all who respond. His demonstration is best known by the relationship between the Almighty Father and His only begotten Son.

Jesus was first loved by the Father before the creation of our world (John 17:24). Who can put a date on this period? No one has a date, but scientists say our world is several billion years old. Consequently, our only focus should be on one fact: The love between God the Father and His Son, along with the Holy Spirit, began prior to the creation. This is therefore the first love relationship in the Godhead, and it points to a never-ending number of love relationships between God and His people. Just as there is no date for the Godhead's love relationship, there is none between God, Adam and Eve. Love remains alive even when His people die. We know eternal life is given to us and that is the only time factor to acknowledge. Christians can enjoy an eternal love relationship with the Godhead.

What can we learn about this love relationship with God? This question alone serves as the beginning of the search for knowledge. I can best understand my relationship with God by first studying the Godhead relationship. The model for the Godhead can be our childhood relationship with parents, since we are created in His image (Genesis 1:26).

The ever-so-popular Scripture of John 3:35 reminds us that the Heavenly Father loves His Son, and the Son loves

His Father (John 14:31). Love never changes between them. We shall never read about hate, resentment or anger in their relationship. We only hope to achieve this same pure love between Him and His people. Many families in the '90s have extreme internal problems attaining this endless love relationship. I do know God wants us to achieve this perfect love through His grace (Matthew 5:43–48). A factor of trust needs some consideration at this time.

John 3:35 not only claims that the Heavenly Father loves His Son, but the Father also delegated all authority over to His Son; nothing other than trust was given by the Father. He knew Jesus would never abuse this trust factor, and Jesus knew His Father would always defend Him. There is a strong bond of commitment to each other. A commitment to this trust factor ensures a strong and reliable comrade in arms, lifelong marriage vows, a noble family lineage, an iron-strength business relationship, and other good things. We can achieve nothing less than trust by the grace and mercy of God's love for us. But of course, there is the cost.

God always has an ultimate spiritual level for us to achieve, and that particular level could cost our life. Jesus knew this was true for Him. This was also one reason for His Father's love toward Him. Jesus knew His death led to a resurrection and eternal life with His Father (John 10:17). Many people find this scenario rather difficult to accept. They would understandably ask, "Why should I die for anyone's love?" A careful study of the Bible will show God's mysteries tend to teach this kind of lifecycle. We can observe that leaves from trees will die, and new leaves return; wild animals live off other animals to survive, just as human consumption includes animals for survival; we eventually die, but our children will carry on our legacy; and finally, God will never allow us to die in vain. The cost of death for God's love does not occur without meaning or purpose. Soldiers died for our freedom, and this action was for an ultimate love of country. Jesus died on the cross for our salvation, and we may die or face another challenge for the love of Christ.

Jesus' second reason for knowing the Father loved Him was from the imagery of love being passed on like a baton to the next person (John 17:26). The concept that God is love was passed on to Jesus. Later on, Jesus passed on the knowledge that God is love to the people. Jesus said His Father's love is in Him, and now that love can be in us. The love that Jesus understood can be verified.[59] Jesus demonstrated knowledge while fasting and being tempted by Satan for forty days. He had healing knowledge and knowledge of being the Son of God at the age of 12. He had the imagery of the baton like love being passed on from one to another. These are very convincing examples about Jesus' knowledge of God's love. Let us consider further the love God has for us.

The Apostle Paul not only claimed nothing would separate the love of Christ from us, but we shall even go beyond being conquerors through Him Who loved us (Romans 8:37). What does his claim actually mean for us? Paul goes on to say in Romans 9:13 (quoting from Malachi 1:2 ff), "Jacob I loved, but Esau I hated." Although a disturbing statement, Paul's premise focused on a message: God has the supreme right to love and hate those He chooses. Paul further claims that we have no right even to challenge God. It is also equally true that God's love can never be changed.

Romans 8:31 actually becomes an answer for verse 37. Paul asked, "If God is for us, who is against us?" God's never-ending love for us ranks higher for Him than for us being conquerors of anyone or anything. Again, His love is eternal and any conquering will only be a temporary event. The subject will always be God, and His people will always be the object of His love whenever we discuss theology. Therefore, the emphasis will always be on what God does for us, and how we respond to Him. We can expect comfort and hope from God.

God's love for us should now be well established in our minds. We also can continue with Paul's lesson from 2 Thessalonians 2:16–17. We could easily use these verses for a benediction during a worship service: "Now may our Lord Jesus Christ Himself and God our Father, who loved us and through grace gave us eternal comfort and good hope, comfort your hearts and strengthen them in every good work and word." Amen. God's love is a continuous process in our lives, giving eternal comfort and hope through grace. We awake each day to a new challenge, and we never know what we shall face that day.

A very popular line in the Forrest Gump movie had a great impact on numerous viewers. Forrest often said, "Life is like a box of chocolates, you never know what you're going to get." Most people claimed that line captured the hearts of many people. No person can deny that simple truth; and yet, a person with a low intelligence, like Forrest Gump, understood life. God reveals Himself to all people, regardless of the IQ factor. We may have perfect health one day and suddenly die the next. We had numerous floods and earthquakes lately; this should be a wake-up call for us. Who can say what we might face each day until it actually comes?

Paul's reminder of God's grace still gives us comfort and good hope, even after a family loses a home from an earthquake. The tragedy can be used to gain stronger faith, which may give wisdom to develop a plan for recovery. It is a time to learn how to exercise one's faith on a positive level. The Bible is truly the Good Word, and comfort does come from reading it. God also sends us messengers to bring good words of instructions and comfort as well. We often hear it said, "God works in mysterious ways and His wonders to perform." We can never be certain how God will work in our lives, but we know He works (Romans 8:28; Galatians 5:6). We only need to trust in Him.

A look at the Old and New Testament will provide us a scriptural basis for the claim of God's work. "For the Lord reproves the one he loves, as a father the son in whom he delights" (Proverbs 3:12). And, "For the Lord disciplines those whom He loves, and chastises every child whom He accepts" (Hebrews 12:6). What instruction can one learn from these two sources? They indeed have an interesting lesson for us. Our lesson reveals God's full awareness of our spiritual weaknesses. We become like Adam and Eve, hiding our doubts of His faithfulness with a cheating heart. We become as deceitful as Ananias and Sapphira (Acts 5:1–6). We can try any of these sinful actions, but God knows it even before we attempt it, since He knows our nature. He simply wants us to know that and be willing to seek forgiveness. We cannot hide sin, but we can learn how to be honest and faithful. These virtues serve us well.

A problem for many people is being a slow learner. They require more discipline to study than others do. They at least come to terms with this, as it relates to God's lessons. A few others, like Ananias and Sapphira, never learn. Peter gave Sapphira many opportunities to confess her sin, but she continued to lie. She even believed the Holy Spirit would not know about their scheme. God cannot love a wicked and scheming heart, but he will always love the person He created. Perhaps His greatest example of truthful love is in His heartbreaking willingness to allow people to make a fatal decision. The good that might come out of such a fatal decision is that some people will learn God's lesson about being honest and faithful to Him. Let us reach the goal of obtaining a pure heart. Paul goes on to teach about making honorable decisions.

A lesson on honorable decisions can come from 2 Corinthians 9:6–7:

> The point is this: the one who sows sparingly will also reap sparingly, and the one who sows bountifully will also reap bountifully. Each of you must give as you made up your mind, not reluctantly or under compulsion, for God loves a cheerful giver.

All that we give in terms of our spirituality and humanity, God expects us to give willingly, cheerfully, with honorable convictions, and with a clear, comprehensive mind. He does not expect any change of decision, nor does He want us to give reluctantly. He loves a cheerful giver instead.

Paul goes to one more level of spiritual growth. Our personal knowledge of good works and our trust in His promises ought to remain as a sufficient reward for us. We should be very grateful when we receive much more than this. A mother and father are often known for being grateful for only seeing a smiling face on their child who has just received a gift. A faithful Christian only needs to know the good that comes from his /her church offerings. When that knowledge becomes more specific, such as 10 baptisms were recently conducted in the new baptismal tank, this Christian will experience a greater joy. The specific knowledge was more than expected. One can conclude that just knowing only good comes from contributions would be the same as sowing sparingly. If God blesses us beyond that knowledge level, it would be known as sowing bountifully. Perhaps this example of spiritual growth underscores how God works in mysterious ways. Let us return to Jesus and how He offers us His love.

The Love of Jesus

How does Jesus show His love for us? Scriptures tend to show Jesus as wanting an active love relationship.[60] Our lesson from these examples is Jesus' requirements from us: make decisions, be committed, extend our energies and show humility.

To Make a Decision

What would happen if neither the man with leprosy nor Jesus ever made a decision (Matthew 8:1–4)? The man obviously decided to kneel before Jesus and claimed that only Jesus' choice could heal him from leprosy. One ought to sense finality in that decision. The healing and the man's choice to trust in Jesus were final and all conclusive. He would remain committed to Jesus.

To Make Commitments

Jesus' last request from His disciple John was to care for Mary as though she was John's mother (John 19:26). Even enduring great amount of pain, Jesus still set a precedent for us all: Complete the final business of your family's welfare before death. We not only make commitments of trust, loyalty and love to our Lord Jesus, but our family receives nothing less. John was equally committed to carrying out Jesus' request. I can hardly think John ever reneged on his commitment. John truly can be admired for extending his energy toward personal commitment for his own family by caring for Mary, Jesus' mother.

Extending Energy for God's Glory

Jesus stilled the storm in order to teach His disciples how to extend their faith (Matthew 8:23–27). The purpose was for God's glory, while the disciples learned a lesson about faith. We must learn that we must go beyond saying we have faith; our lives must prove it. Jesus' disciples felt that being awake was the only way to be much help in any crisis. They had to trust in God's divine protection, and since Jesus is the Son of God, His presence was all that was necessary. We can only show our commitment to this statement of faith by extending our faith. Let us consider more scripture verses that support this notion.

Jesus commands us to "abide in my love" since the Father loved Jesus just as Jesus loved us (John 15:9). The Apostle Paul made two contentions: (a) Christ lives in Paul since Jesus was crucified with Paul, and (b) Paul lives "by faith in the Son of God, who loved me and gave Himself for me" (Galatians 2:20). Paul also said we ought to be imitators of God and walk in love as "a fragrant offering and sacrifice to God" (Ephesians 5:1–2). How would you respond to these scriptures? We simply extend our energies as far as we can. We all know that any fragrance can extend itself and have an effect on other objects. Our faith must have the same effect on other people, and it may require some sacrifice. There is absolutely no place for negative blemishes in our lives. However, this does not include natural negative feelings coming from medical sufferings or a loss of loved ones but, rather, negative blemishes include resentment or the hatred of others. We can only depend on

God's grace for an energetic extension of our faith to survive. The final demonstration of an active love relationship is humility.

Humility

It took tough love for Jesus to help a wealthy young man understand humility. Jesus said, "You lack one thing; go, sell what you have, and give to the poor, and you will have treasure in heaven; and come, follow me" (Mark 10:21). No one is really in a position to quickly judge this young man. It is much easier for me to say that all Christians are willing to profess their faith, than it is to claim that all Christians are more humble than that wealthy young man. Perhaps I can also easily say that a much higher percentage of Christians are like the wealthy young man than those who are humble. Wealth means security for most people. We are all reminded about this when the retired senior citizens rightfully fight for the security of their pensions; when young people rightfully say they do not expect any Social Security benefits, even though they have and will be paying into that fund; when the majority of citizens live in fear of crime and corruption, so much that their front doors have at least three locks and their windows have bars on them; and when our politicians mismanage our tax dollars to the point that they now say we might not get our money from our savings bonds.

What did Jesus mean? I am not convinced Jesus wants all Christians to sell all their wealth (1 Samuel 2:7; Ecclesiastes 5:19) as I am convinced that He wants me to commit my whole life to Jesus (Psalms 49:6–7). God has never refused His people wealth, but He will refuse the assentation of our sins (Proverbs 18:11; 28:11; Luke 12:19). Our weakness can be in our values.

Each person will develop a value system by which to live. We just learned humility shows how wealth can either destroy one's faith or make it stronger. It depends on one's value of wealth. We are also weak when pride, resentment and hate enter into our value system. Admitting to wrong actions can be a humbling experience. We all have that experience one time or another. Thank God we eventually are confronted for being resentful, having too much pride and for showing hatred toward other people. He does it only because He loves us. We can now come to the conclusion of Jesus' love for us by confessing that Jesus is Lord.

Confess that Jesus Is Lord

Our next lesson and example of Jesus' love for is a confession that He is Lord.[61] Confession is good for the soul; it always has been, and it will continue to be.[62] Our confessions are therefore anchored in Christian faith and are never to be taken lightly. I witnessed a young soldier, who suffered from a serious Jeep accident, go into total calmness after his confession and hearing my prayer. His doctor requested a chaplain before the lad went into surgery. Perhaps this soldier's experience will demonstrate that confessions must go beyond lip service. Our belief that Jesus is Lord must be obvious to the outsiders of the faith. People must witness this statement of faith from our appearance, our lifestyle, our conversations, our display of attitude and our total being. Our confession should be a reminder that Jesus will always remain faithful to us.

We can learn from the four Gospels that Jesus never changed his steadfast love for His disciples and was always supportive.[63] We can also learn about Jesus' support by reading these four Gospels. He will meet our needs. Let us now learn how to practice love.

Practice Love

What can we learn from the Supernatural Beings about the practice of love? The goal is to prove one's love, even while under fire from critics. The Godhead can be a model for us again. We ought to follow the advice of 1 John 3:18: "My little children, let us not love in word, or in tongue, but in word and truth."

What do you think is meant by word and truth? I think of God, reverence, Holy, power, honesty, freedom, integrity, sincerity, dignity, pain, suffering, death and much more. Jesus experienced all these and even more. We should follow His example as presented in these four Gospels.

John 13:1, 34

I often heard it said about the knowledge of another person: You cannot know that person well unless you wear his/her shoes. In light of that assertion, can we wear the sandals of Jesus? Can we walk as He walked in accordance with His Father's will? The writer of John 13 offers this particular challenge to all of us. He essentially wrote that Jesus commands us to love one another as He loves us, until we die. He expects us to treat others as though He actually lives in our body, as if He is listening while we talk. We should conduct our relationships with others as though we are actually Jesus Himself (Matthew 10:40–42).

This forces us to ask, What would Jesus say at this point? The writer of Matthew 25:35–40 continues with a little twist by saying: When we fed the poor, we fed Him (Jesus); when we visited the sick, we visited with Him; when we called on someone in prison, we called on Him; or when someone was naked and we gave him or her clothing, we gave Jesus clothing. These examples place us in a position of actually serving Jesus Himself. The face of Jesus is seen on both the recipient and the servant. We must do these things as long as we live. Although these examples represent positive views, let us consider some negative views from the Old Testament.

We can find the negative views in Psalms 78:36–37. God's people mocked Him with their mouth and tongue, and they were not faithful in His covenant. The people in Psalms 78 did not show love and respect, nor can we witness it today. Many people are able to flatter and lie to others in any given moment. They even do it without the blink of an eye. Our twentieth-century society developed parallel lines of communication: Flattering is the top line, and lying is the bottom line. This is offensive to God, and nothing less is true when we do it to others. I often ask myself how much worse this will be in the twenty-first century. Perhaps there is hope after reading Psalms 77:1, 3. "My voice [is] to God, and I cry; my voice [is] to God, and He listened to me.…I remembered God and am troubled; I meditate and my spirit faints. Selah." We find sincerity in the very depths of the Psalmist's soul.

Personally, I need to draw from my own experiences to better understand the seriousness and urgency of these two verses. As I do, my thoughts recall two professors at one of the three seminaries I attended. They felt I was not able to achieve the academic excellence they decided would be acceptable. Their confrontation was equally insensitive. I privately cried out to God for spiritual strength and hoped that I was truly in His will. God listened and offered me hope. Amen. Our personal reflections will draw us into a solemn identity with scriptures of hope; it becomes a positive practice of love.

THE PERSON LOVED BY GOD

What can we learn from the Supernatural Beings about the person loved by God? We ultimately become a participant in divine love as a direct result of God's love for us (1 John 4:7–21). We therefore experience a true point of contact between God and ourselves. We are like God when we are kind and loving toward others; when our love contains its own sense of obligation; when we love God with all our heart, soul, mind and strength (Mark 12:29–30); and when we love our neighbors as ourselves (Mark 12:31). God loved His people in the past just as much as He does today and will in the future. We need to understand God's simple-and-yet-profound formula in the language describing His love. The formula includes God's own time (past, present and future); God's people who continuously abide in God's love; and a spiritual relationship, which was first received by Moses and later by Jesus for God's people. This formula is a gift of salvation from God the Father. It is a true expression of divine love. We have every reason to praise the glory and grace of God, which He gave us as His beloved (Ephesians 1:6). "All nations can be joint heirs, and of the same body, and sharers of His promise in Christ, through the gospel" (3:6). We must be eager for the unity of the Spirit in the bond of peace (4:3). And finally, praise Jesus for "having ascended on high, He led captivity captive, and gave gifts to men" (4:8).

The word gave actually means received, just as written in Exodus 31:18: "And He gave to Moses, as He finished speaking with him on the mountain of Sinai, the two tablets of testimony, tablets of stone, written with the finger of God." The theology clearly teaches us that both Moses and Jesus received the tablets from the Father, and both spent fourty days and fourty nights away from the people. Moses received the Law for the people to obey in order to receive salvation from sin. On the other hand, Jesus received all authority from His Father to remove our bondage of total sin and to place sin somewhere in the "Twilight Zone" of captivity. It appears Paul successfully linked Moses with Jesus.

The Old and New Testament are linked together by Moses and Jesus. All of God's promises fall in their proper places of logic when Moses and Jesus are linked together. This was Paul's reason for saying we are joint heirs and sharers of the Heavenly Father's promise of the Christ. This also becomes our reason to praise God, for being His favorite beloved and for us to be eagerly keeping the unity of the Spirit in the bond of peace. And finally, this is also the reason we accept Christ and, consequently, became God's elect and beloved (Deuteronomy 32:15; 33:5, 26; Isaiah 44:2). We must never forget this promise and that God's love always remains steadfast for us.

People do forget, "But Jeshurum [a people] grew fat, and wicked, you grew fat, thick, [and] stubborn; and he abandoned God who made him, and dishonored the Rock of His Salvation" (Deuteronomy 32:15). The author offers us a very strong implication of people getting out of control—forgetting their salvation and bond of peace. Again, Jeshurum refers to God's upright, well-informed believers, or an honorable people of God. They became rich in the knowledge of God and their faith. They became like Adam and Eve, enduring exploitations from Satan (Genesis 3:5). These people knew right from wrong but chose the wrong way. Life will always include struggles, but God will give us inner strength to overcome them with a well-balanced faith.

Jesus once said, "It will be hard for a rich man [or woman] to enter the kingdom of heaven" (Matthew 19:23). Neither by flattery or lying, nor by money or official power will ever a person's humility develop. On the other hand, neither resentment nor vindictive actions due to poverty will ever develop a person's humility. Instead, humility comes from the very depth of our soul and is sincerely displayed by our words, actions and body language. The rich and poor can learn this lesson well. The rich have all the wealth and comfort to deal with, but the poor have only the grace of God to depend on. Perhaps Jesus felt the poor were under much less pressure than the rich, since they never had the wealth and comfort to make them complacent. The rich can easily fall into the trap of seeking God only for their convenience, while the poor are drawn closer to God out of deprivation. The poor will always find hope for peace and salvation from oppression, but the rich must learn that their wealth was given by the grace of God for them to manage and share with the poor. God does offer a balance for both the rich and poor.

The Apostle Paul offers the following suggestion: "Then put on as the elect of God, holy and beloved, tender feelings of mercy, kindness, humility, meekness, longsuffering…" (Colossians 3:12). "But we ought to thank God always concerning you, brothers, beloved by [the] Lord, because God chose you from the beginning to salvation in sanctification of [the] Spirit and belief of the Truth" (2 Thessalonians 2:13). Both the rich and the poor can be holy and beloved because of God's grace, and He lives in them. In conclusion, the rich must never forget where wealth comes; and equally true, the poor must never forget Who offers hope and salvation during deprivation. Both are expected to trust in God.

God does teach mercy, kindness, humility, meekness and longsuffering through the life of Jesus. We must learn how to trust in God to perfect these virtues in our own lives. Perhaps the key scripture is 2 Thessalonians, where Paul urges all people to "thank God always concerning you, brothers, beloved by [the] Lord." Our thanks and gratitude somehow increases our trust in God. We need to learn how we can thank God in our prayers, the way we walk, in our manner, from our treatment of others, in our motives for any actions and in everything. Helping others might be ideal for some people, but God wants us to make it a reality. Misfortunes will happen.

God gets blamed for any misfortune with the rich or poor. No one has the count on the number of people who have blamed God. Some theologians claim that God wants to remove that rebellious heart so misfortunes will never be blamed on God. Revelation 20:9–10 tells us:

> They marched up over the breadth of the earth and surrounded the camp of the saints and the beloved city. And fire came down from heaven and consumed them. And the devil who had deceived them was thrown into the lake of fire and sulfur, where the beast and the false prophet were, and they will be tormented day and night forever and ever.

Satan and his devils are to be blamed for all misfortunes. Instead, people with numerous misfortunes become rebellious enough to blame God and not the devil. It is therefore unfortunate that Revelation 20 appears to claim that both God's people who have been deceived and the devil's would be thrown into the fire and sulfur. The late Dr. George E. Ladd, professor at Fuller Theological Seminary and author of numerous books, was truly correct with this statement: "The ultimate root of sin is not poverty or inadequate social conditions or an unfortunate environment; it is the rebelliousness of the human heart." God consumed sin and not the good in His people. The imagery can be somewhat compared with Moses' command of the sons of Levi to kill their brother, friend and neighbor who sinned against God (Exodus 32:25–29). About 3,000 people were slain that day. What causes a person to become rebellious from the heart?

We are, by nature, a people with inquisitive minds for adventure. The distance we travel on this adventure is determined by the degree of our own vanity. Each person determines the distance. Revelation 20:1–15 describes an incredible challenge for God's people to accept. One thousand years of total peace without evil will occur. I can only speculate on the distance people with an inquisitive mind will travel. I would think a person with this inquisitive mind would ultimately become totally bored over total peace. I suggest this result only because the Scripture is silent about a person's mindset during these 1,000 years. Revelation 20 simply tells us that Satan deceives numerous people after he is released from the pit. This information tells me that a person's nature did not change during the 1,000 years.

We finally must conclude that each person must decide when and where to stop traveling on the road of adventure that includes Satan's clever temptations. We must also realize that the lake of fire and sulfur is the place where sinful people will go, even though God created it for Satan and other fallen angels. The Apostle Paul reminds us in Romans 9:25–29 of the following: God will call "my people" and the "beloved" whom He chooses. All remnants of the faithful will be saved from this lake of fire and sulfur.

The Horizontal Love Relationship

We completed the vertical love relationship for the purpose of it as a foundation for the horizontal love relationship. We now move from the question of why and how God reveals love, and our response to it, and go to a consideration of ways we can express love between one another. The process encourages our honest and earnest involvement. Let us begin with the meaning of affection.

Cherished Love

There is something very special and yet very righteous as well about a cherished love that enhances benevolent affection. We know righteous benevolent affection comes from God, and since that is true, then God's love is the kernel within a cherished love. God shows benevolent affection toward His people. He cherishes that love for His people, and it is therefore central in the concept of benevolent affection for others. We shall now consider seven examples that show how God wants His people to show love toward others.

1. **Love others more than yourself.** There is no greater example of this than the love between husband and wife. The Apostle Paul dealt with this issue in Ephesians 5:25–33 and Colossians 3:19. Paul first told husbands to love their wives as Christ loves His church. Although Jesus died for our sins and therefore died for His church, Paul most likely meant that husbands must remain with their wives until death. Unfortunately the news media has reported elderly couples committing suicide to avoid being a burden to their children. Also, there is an elderly man in Florida who is serving prison time for killing his Alzheimer's wife. This is truly a sad commentary on our civilized society. These

elderly people may have died in a tragic way, but one cannot deny they truly had love for one another.

I was once told about a husband who stopped a bullet that was originally meant for his wife. It proved to be a political situation, and the story was quite involved. No one knows when or how one will be forced into any situation that will take away a life. We only know it becomes an ultimate expression of love for the one who dies so another person can live.

Husbands, we have considered only the extreme examples of love. You also have other options: be a teacher, a healer, a provider or simply be a friend to your wives. Your sensitivity to her needs is all she expects.

2. **Love others as your own body.** The Bible commands us to love our neighbors as ourselves.[64]

Who is our neighbor? I would consider the families in our Stoney Creek Apartments as neighbors, or the person sitting next to me in church, the person who works with me, or simply anyone I meet. I have a sense of concern and respect for my neighbor, as I do for my own body. If I have no respect and concern for myself, then how can I ever expect to show that to others? The extreme of having absolutely no respect and concern for myself would be if I destroy myself physically, socially, psychologically, economically, politically and theologically. There is no love for anyone at this point.

There are both Christians and non-Christians who apparently do not love their neighbors. I often send out signals of this observation by immediately reaching for my wallet whenever a businessman tells me that he is a Christian. I also search for another businessman. I know how to protect myself even when businessmen make no such claims. This is nothing less than a very sad commentary on Christians who claim they love their neighbors.

We could tell many more stories like mine. As for me, I noticed one common truth, which always remains apparent: We shall all experience both evil and good. Evil tends to show its ugly head more than good. Our Lord had a very good reason for commanding that we love our neighbor as our own body. This extension of love from one's self to others will ultimately overcome evil. However, we must do something else first.

3. **Love the Lord with all your heart, soul and mind.** No one can even begin to love others more than their self without one important knowledge of truth: Almighty God commands us to love the Lord with all our heart, soul and mind.[65] God will allow me some space and time to develop an understanding and strength to love Him. Each person is on his/her own timetable. No one can judge how much others are able to develop understanding and strength, since only Almighty God has this authority. We actually love the Lord by exulting and glorifying God Himself (1 Peter 1:8). We achieve this level of love when we are able to love the Lord only through our belief in Him (Matthew 22:37; Romans 8:28). Jesus brought this point out when He asked Thomas to touch His wounds (John 20:24–29). Our Lord is exalted and glorified when we are able to love Him through our belief. This finally demonstrates that we love the Lord with all our heart, soul and mind. We can go beyond by reaching out to others. Now, Jesus commands another requirement.

4. **Christians, love your enemies.** Jesus commands us to love our enemies, bless those who curse and hate us, and

pray for those who abuse and persecute us (Matthew 5:44; Luke 6:27–35). We can hastily agree that we have gone beyond loving others more than self by loving our enemies. This is an incredible command. I always find it impossible to do this with my own energy. Only God can love others through me. His love will be enough for my enemies and me. I have all I can take dealing with my soul, which is very troubled with all the evil my enemies force upon me. Only God works through me to love my enemies. His strength becomes my strength to achieve this command.

Who are the enemies? We are now entering into a phase of paranoia truth. I never actually used this phrase to describe an actual mood that occurs in our lives. Any person who describes the kind of mood, which I plan to introduce, will indeed appear quite paranoid. The mindset of present society, as we enter the twenty-first century, commands total denial of the following facts:

a) Christians are known to curse, hate, abuse and persecute others they find to be repugnant.
b) Clergies are known to belie the integrity, reputation and intelligence of other clergy.
c) Christian businessmen and women are known for exploiting the innocence of other Christians.

I never met a Christian who would agree that these claims actually occurred. I am always told that I must have misunderstood. I had a secretary who often told me I was paranoid. If this is difficult to accept, there is another more difficult claim to make.

We have laws protecting criminals against innocent victims.

- A landowner can go to jail if that person shoots a thief breaking into his/her home.
- A person can go to jail for shooting criminals in self-defense.
- A wife can go to jail for shooting her husband who criminally abused her.

The list continues. Where is our civilized society heading? God wants us to love and pray for our enemies. It is only by the grace and love of God, which works through me, that my enemies are loved. I truly believe God accepts this prayer from me. Amen.

5. **Owe only love to one another.** The Apostle Paul desperately tried to change the meaning of owing others (Romans 13:8). The majority of people will only attach a monetary value to owing others. Paul apparently did not approve of owing money to others. There are other scriptures giving the importance of loving others: "If you love those who love you, what reward do you have?" (Matthew 5:46). "...Even sinners do the same" (Luke 6:32). "The one loving his brother rests in the light" (1 John 2:10; 3:10, 14; 4:19–20; 5:2). Love for others only has good at work in our lives.

Love for others will inspire a willingness to pay taxes, obey all laws, commit no adultery or murder, avoid stealing or bearing false witness, or simply not doing anything against the will of God. The point of all of this is this that we only owe others our love and good deeds. We love others without any exception or anything in return. We only offer unconditional love.

6. **Love must rest in the light.** The concept of light was brought out in John 1:4–9 and 1 John 1:5–10. Theologians taught us in their writings that light brings knowledge and understanding to the world concerning the mind of God. One of many lessons for the world to learn is on *dualism*—good and evil, love and hate, and peace and war. We apparently shall always witness two opposing forces in our world. Jesus taught us that one cannot serve two masters (Matthew 6:24; Luke 16:13). Perhaps Jesus was thinking about the Old Testament story about a man with two wives (Deuteronomy 21:15–17). This story tells about a man hating his wife who had his firstborn child and loving another wife with his second-born child. The man's dilemma was over who must receive the double portion of inheritance—the first or second born. The situation taught a valuable lesson: One must choose one wife and Lord, and only serve truth. Life becomes complicated even without such a dilemma. The more we seek this light, the more knowledge and understanding we gain about good and evil, love and hate, and what's true and false.

7. **Loving more may cause less love for me.** Recognition is a healthy response to people who serve well in any endeavor. Unfortunately, a few well-deserving people are forgotten more times than they are remembered. One well-deserving church organist in the military rarely received recognition for playing beautiful music and donating her time. Other organists, who are paid, often received recognition along with being able to attend workshops for organists. Few chaplains decided to bring shame upon those people in authority for their insensitivity toward the more unfortunate organist. This is an obvious example of people

who share the most love and yet are loved less (Luke 7:47; 2 Corinthians 12:15). The Apostle Paul enjoyed serving others without recognition and so did Mary, the sister of Lazarus, who showed love for Jesus (John 12:1–8). This does not say their recognition is something to ignore. Christians ought to become the primary examples of showing well-balanced love distribution among givers and receivers of love.

Any staff member working with substance-abuse patients will tell you that they give 100 percent of their energy expecting no more than 10 percent in return. I have been amazed at the amount of love they show these patients, who seldom express any form of appreciation; they only complain. These professionals deserve recognition, but they seldom get it. I know a psychologist who eventually received a medical retirement for being totally burnt out. Most of his recognition later were letters of reprimand. He also never received a farewell party. Only shame should be given to those in authority since this particular discipline of psychology actually teaches the value of love for others. I never understood why this staff member received such a lack of sensitivity. The only surviving thing for this psychologist is a message on hope. He will find that hope, peace and self worth from our Lord, Who surely knows about lack of recognition.

Conclusion

Love first comes from God. He spent thousands of years sharing His love before He finally sent His only begotten Son to teach us more about His love. Theologians will all agree that Jesus, Who is God's Son, revealed a great example of the love we ought to receive and share with others. The vertical love relationship needs to be understood before we can go on to express our own horizontal love relationship with one another. We may well spend a lifetime learning about this love.

Addendum Five

A Theological Approach to Power and the Holy Spirit

A practical theological understanding of both power and the Holy Spirit ultimately requires a distinct, separate conceptualization and interpretation. We, the people of God, are often greeted with contemporary confusion relative to the separate roles. A simple survey of Acts will reveal the classic Greek use of natural and supernatural powers:

> So when they had come together, they asked Him, "Lord, will you at this time restore the kingdom to Israel?" He said to them, "It is not for you to know times or seasons which the Father has fixed by His own authority. But you shall receive power when the Holy Spirit has come upon you; and you shall be my witnesses in Jerusalem

> and in all Judea and Samaria and to the end of the earth." (Acts 1:6–8)
>
> When the day of Pentecost had come, they were all together in one place. And suddenly a sound came from heaven like the rush of a mighty wind, and it filled all the house where they were sitting. And there appeared to them tongues as of fire, distributed and resting on each one of them. And they were all filled with the Holy Spirit and began to speak in other tongues, as the Spirit gave them utterance. (2:1–4)

A Contemporary Confusion about Power

One can learn how to make a distinction between natural and supernatural powers; one begins by not equalizing both powers. The supernatural will always overcome the natural, putting the natural power in the "Lost and Found." Perhaps a fundamental example can be a claim that a twenty-mile run is achieved only by God's supernatural power. You say that it never happens? Some Christians have said it. Truly, credit can only be granted to one's innate, natural power of determination and the God-given energy to practice. Now then, what can be said for an 80-year-old man running and winning that twenty-mile race? It would naturally say very little about the younger contenders; but perhaps supernatural power intervenes only for the glory of God. It would serve mostly as a fulfillment of the private hope and a reminder of the past victories this elderly man had accomplished. The abnormal prevailed over the natural.

A Conceptualization of Power

Natural and supernatural powers were already mentioned. Luke, the author of Acts, formed two Greek words that support our English words. Luke's references to the natural (innate) power are found in Acts 4:16, 20; 5:39; 8:31; 10:47; 13:39; 15:1; 17:19; 19:40; 20:32; 21:34; 24:8, 11, 13; 25:11; 26:32; 27:12, 15, 31, 39, 43.[66] These references appear to support an innate, daily condition among the people.

Part A

Luke used the supernatural (miraculous) power in Acts 1:8; 2:22; 3:12; 4:7, 33; 6:8; 8:10, 13; 10:38; 19:11.[67] They all came from God the Father. Jesus even claimed that He received His power from the Father (Acts 10:38).

Part B

Luke also used this supernatural power in the sense of a delegation of authority, ability, privilege, commission or control: Acts 1:7; 5:4; 8:19; 9:14; 26:10,12, 18.[68] One tends to employ the phrase: "A covering by divine authority," to describe this process of delegation. Jesus delegated the power of the Holy Spirit to those who were filled with the Holy Spirit (Acts 1:8; 2:4).

Interpreting Natural Power

Luke wrote this word to interpret the meaning of "being able" as a God-given, innate power to use for thinking through a process or to carry out a course of action. Peter and John used their innate power for their answer to the council: "For we cannot but speak of what we have seen and heard" (Acts 4:20). Peter and John simply told what they saw and heard from Jesus. On the other hand, Philip was able to interpret the meaning of an Old Testament scripture in Isaiah to help the Ethiopian eunuch (Acts 8:31, 37). Authority was delegated to Philip so he and the eunuch could experience God working within their study. A person does not always go beyond his/her own God-given ability to begin witnessing; but when that ends, divine power takes over. It seems to me that all Olympic athletes could represent those people who have witnessed their own innate and limited power; similar to a cancer patient who continues to live until there is no longer than one minute left to breathe. God takes over at the time of death or at the time when He chooses to extend that cancer patient's life.

Interpreting Supernatural Power

In Acts, Luke provides ten different occasions when supernatural power was used. I shall interpret only these four:

1. The supernatural power in bearing witness (Acts 4:8–12).
2. The supernatural power in the Lordship and Messiahship (2:22).
3. The supernatural power in the name of Jesus (3:12; 4:7).
4. The supernatural power of transformation (4:33).

Bearing Witness

Being filled with the Holy Spirit, Peter bore witness to the supernatural healing of the crippled man that was done in the name and power of Jesus (Acts 4:8–12). We should now recognize that authority was delegated to Peter on this occasion. He operated under the same authority as Jesus because God the Father willed it. Peter experienced the same power as Jesus during this healing, but Peter was limited to whatever power was delegated. You and I can share in this same experience.[69] We are therefore called to a witness-bearing mission just as Jesus' apostles were (Acts

2:32; 3:14; 5:32; 10:39; 13:31; 22:15). Dr. William S. LaSor commented in his book, *Church Alive*:[70] "During the present age it is our responsibility to take what He gives [power of the Holy Spirit], and to be what He wants us to be [His witnesses]."

Lordship and Messiahship

The power seen and experienced in Jesus is a sign of God's will. The same holds true for the apostles. The resurrection of Jesus, the Lordship or Messiahship of Jesus, and the miracles performed by His apostles merely define more clearly the powers of God. Consequently, the fact that God wills something to occur, or commands it, is itself the origin of such power. As an overview: one begins with God's will, passes through His heavenly power—experiences a miracle and/or spiritually changed into a new man—receives the power of the Holy Spirit and then witnesses to others with and about this power. The Lordship and Messiahship represent the covering of God's authority and power and God's will for it to be.

The Name of Jesus

God willed that all authority and power be given to Jesus (John 5:27). The spoken name of Jesus possesses heavenly powers since God willed this to be. A person simply says, "In the name of Jesus," as Peter did (Acts 3:6). Peter told his hearers that the name of Jesus enabled the cripple to spring up to his feet and walk; that miracle clearly defined God's power. The future of that cripple man became inextricably bound to God's will. His destiny in his history was to walk. God pronounced this man healed through the voice of Peter, and God does not contradict Himself or go back on His word.

God also said that the Israelites are His people and that salvation is offered to Israel through Jesus. A divine foreknowledge of God inextricably binds Israel into salvation. Israel's destiny is to accept salvation through Jesus. If Israel continues to refuse salvation, as implied in Acts 3:23, then she will be involved in total destruction. Just as history tells us that many Jews have already accepted Jesus as their salvation, there are also nonbelievers, such as Gentiles, who do not accept Jesus. Every knee must bow and every mouth must confess that Jesus is Lord and the way of salvation (Philippians 2:10–11).

Transformation

Among all apostles, supernatural power was at work to heal the sick and to transform self-centered individuals into self-sacrificing members of a society (Acts 3:43–47; 4:32–37). A very important aspect of the moral and spiritual change in the lives of believers requires our special attention. A remarkable unanimity existed within that Spirit-filled community. The poor had no need since there was the common sharing of possessions among the believers. The change was an answer to prayer when the Holy Spirit came upon the group for another filling (Acts 4:30–31). God truly transforms His people.

Miracles Performed through Power

How do we witness in the Holy Spirit? If one should happen to study verse 8, the word power leaps out. Jesus promised that His disciples would receive power from the Holy Spirit. Further study shows that this promise is extended to all Christians.[71] All powers are a gift from God Almighty when He chooses to give them.[72]

Offering us the experience of His power through the Holy Spirit and His people is for our needs and not for God. Our spiritual growth becomes the object of God's intent and purpose.[73] Let us now separate the super and natural powers by a more definitive focus on the Holy Spirit.

The Creative Role of the Holy Spirit

Understanding of the birth of Jesus and its symbolism is found in the creative power of the Holy Spirit. The premise for this supernatural claim is also found in the following scripture: "She was found to be with child by the Holy Spirit" (Matthew 1:18). It was a supernatural conception. Indeed, the Holy Spirit is the creative power of God that first fashioned the life of Jesus, just as the creative thoughts of contemporary writers are secondarily fashioned today. Both are empowered by the Holy Spirit.

Perhaps the Apostle Paul was on to something in 2 Corinthians 3:12–18 and 12:2–10. Paul teaches about a special kind of freedom one experiences with the Holy Spirit. Chapter 3 is symbolic of a free mind, which offers hope to act boldly for the glory of God. Chapter 12 is also symbolic of hope, with the conviction that God truly knows our free thoughts and the fact that our actions are empowered by the Holy Spirit. Only God the Father knows this to be absolutely true, and it should never become a matter of concern whether others ever find out. My human weakness causes a personal struggle over the reality that no one may ever know about my pure thoughts and actions; or if they do know, they may never trust or believe me. It will be times like this when the Holy Spirit gives the grace of freedom to never worry, since God truly knows and loves us. This is all that should matter. God chose to give us this freedom a long time ago.

We must read the following scripture: "And the Spirit of the Lord shall rest upon him, the Spirit of wisdom and understanding, the Spirit of counsel and might, the Spirit of knowledge and the fear of the Lord" (Isaiah 11:2). God's choice is for all to believe in this scripture as the word of God for all His people, regardless of the time or season. It is because of God's lovingkindness that He continuously shares the Holy Spirit with us.

In light of God's lovingkindness, we are all given a new beginning or new chance in life by the help of the Holy Spirit. He heals the sexually assaulted woman from all her pain. He gives grace to parents during their loss of an infant. He offers peace and sanity over the insanity of 250 lives being snuffed out from a highly explosive bomb. He empowers a medical doctor to rescue an overdose patient. The list continues. The Holy Spirit simply reaches down to anyone who calls for help, and He offers the glory of God's lovingkindness. He restructures a broken heart, body and mind by making them new. Thanks be to God the Father, Son and Holy Spirit. Amen.

Addendum Six

A Theological, Sociological and Psychological Look at Divorce

Divorce is a tragedy for all members of a family. One will wonder why it happens; or worse, why did it happen to us? The answer never comes easily. Families slowly and painfully suffer through the personal journey of recovery, each journey uniquely its own. The process each family chooses will ultimately determine how well the recovery will be. The following points hopefully offer a reasonable and successful guidance for recovery. Let us begin with a theological look at divorce.

The Theology of Divorce

Theology is a study that asks what God would do concerning His fellowship with His people. The key to understanding theology is in God's mind. We must therefore make our own humble attempt to look respectively in and through God's mind and eyes. Already, our interpretation will be a conjecture at best. The words of God found in our Bible are our best reliable source.

We begin with theology and suddenly find ourselves looking at the Holy Bible as a reliable source. I contend that our interpretation of God's mind and eye can only come from the Bible. We shall now ask ourselves what both the Old and New Testament reveals in reliable facts about God's mind and eye.

Jesus suffered for and trusted in His Father as our Precedent for a partnership suited to God the Father (Genesis 2:18; Hebrews 2:11–13). God began the process of defining His partnership by creating Adam and Eve. The process continues until the Son of God takes charge of it. The Heavenly Father wants His people to understand the meaning and purpose of His partnership.

Ironically, there is also a partnership within the Godhead, and the same is true for the human race. Jesus, as the Son of God, was given the mandate to communicate how the divine partnership functions, and all people would then learn what should occur in that partnership. Since Jesus is in the Godhead, we can understand why suffering and trusting are the two most important ingredients for a solid partnership. We should also understand, then, why all partnerships exist for the glory of God. Let us now carry these truths, which we should believe with all our heart, soul and mind, and look at the Old and New Testament.

THE OLD-TESTAMENT TESTIMONY

The first three verses of Deuteronomy 24 represent the introduction, and verse four contains the main conditional clause. God revealed that divorce was not mandatory or approved of when the wife does something objectionable and is found out by her husband. Rather, God demands this husband to not take his wife back if she decides to marry another man, and that second marriage fails. In the days of Moses' law, divorce was apparently permitted and tolerated to the extent that no civil or ecclesiastical penalty was imposed.

Divorce was practiced in terms of a permission since it was tolerated to the extent that no civil or ecclesiastical penalty was imposed.[74] There was no certain claim that unseemly behavior would allow divorce; and it definitely was not adultery—death was the penalty for such behavior (cf. Leviticus 20:10; Deuteronomy 22:22–27). Nor could adultery be suspected without proof (cf. Numbers 5:11–31). Another provisions can be found in Deuteronomy 22:13–29: A man who marries a woman, and later decides that he does not like her, has the right to begin a process to slander his new wife by claiming she was not a virgin before their marriage. Please note that the cause is the loss of virginity prior to marriage, and the judgment is what we now call annulment.

This whole study on partnership began with Adam and Eve. We can dimly comprehend what occurs in the Godhead when we consider the partnership between Adam and Eve. Unfortunately, we have very little data to review. I would like to suggest that verse 18 from Genesis 2:18–24 gives us something to chew on: "It is not good that man should be alone; I will make him a helper as his partner." The Living Bible Version went on to interpret partner as "a helper suited for his needs." This language obviously elevates the man since Eve was placed under Adam's command. The term partnership can now be understood to reflect the image of the Godhead—the Heavenly Father commands His Son, and, being under the Father's authority, Jesus commands the Holy Spirit.

Unfortunately, the 1990s have created a confrontation to this concept. But, rather than focusing on man's authority over the woman, a solution could be in the word commitment. We can know God's commitment to His people and His expectation for our commitment to Him. God is glorified in all He does for His people and in what all his people do for Him. God wanted this kind of partnership between Adam and Eve. God's commitment to their partnership shows some compassion when Eve later gives birth to Seth, which means granted or appointed. Out of their suffering, Adam and Eve learned how to trust in God's authority and commitment.

We now must understand that the Heavenly Father's involvement in such a partnership was turned over to the Son of God. The Heavenly Father glories in His Son's partnership with the human race. This is now a partnership suited for Christ Jesus; we, therefore, must study the New Testament for further insight. We cannot find any more helpful information than what we already have in the Old Testament.

The New-Testament Testimony

Let's review teachings from Jesus about divorce in these following scriptures: Matthew 5:31–32; 19:3–9; Mark 10: 2-12; Luke 16:18. Please note that Mark 10:12 includes an offending husband, otherwise we read that the wife commits adultery whenever she remarries. A divorce is permitted in these cases. The only exception for remarriage is the discovery of sexual intercourse prior to marriage by a spouse (Matthew 5:32; 19:9). A man or woman being divorced for the reason of one spouse committing adultery is not permitted.[75] The bottom line is that Jesus approved divorce based on adultery by one of the spouse, but He did not allow them to remarry. He also did not make divorce mandatory. Herein is where Jesus separated from the Old Testament Law on divorce. He subsequently offers permission for an annulment. The innocent victim/spouse has the right to remarry.

The Apostle Paul taught that the death of a spouse dissolves a marriage; therefore the surviving partner could remarry (Romans 7:1–3; 1 Corinthians 7:39). The Apostle Paul also claimed that the Lord does not approve of divorced Christians remarrying, but hopes for their reconciliation (1 Corinthians 7:10–11). However, he did approve of letting an unbeliever separate from a Christian spouse. Again, a Christian who agrees to marry an unbeliever cannot divorce, since this action makes their children become unclean. He also claimed that a Christian makes the unbelieving spouse holy (1 Corinthians 7:12–15). Let us consider a few partnerships.

The Partnership Suited for Christ

The Pharisees confronted Jesus on the question of divorce: "Is it lawful for a man to divorce his wife?"

He answered them, "What did Moses command you?"

They said, "Moses allowed a man to write a certificate of dismissal and to divorce her."

But Jesus said to them, "Because of your hardness of heart he wrote this commandment for you" (Mark 10:2–5). The following verses not only supported partnership but concluded with these words, "Therefore what God has joined together, let no one separate" (10: 9). Jesus ultimately prefers a lifelong partnership with us. He wants us to reconcile all our differences that will become very serious issues in the marriage.

We find a new example for partnership in Mark 10:13–16. The message here is the following: God the Father gave His people over to His Son Jesus as His children to receive salvation, become heirs of God's kingdom and coheirs with Christ. This briefly describes a solid example of a lifelong partnership suited for Christ. We get our scriptural support of this claim from Mark 10:14, "Let the little children come to me; do not stop them; for it is to such as these that the kingdom of God belongs." We often restrict this command from Jesus to His relationship with little children. Although this is generally true, a warning signal in our head needs to sound off from the phrase kingdom of God. There is a theological message here: The very moment a person accepts Christ as Lord and Savior, he or she is considered as a child of God—a child whom the Heavenly Father has turned over to His Son. There is no age limit in this case, be it 50, 60 or even 80 years old when one accepts Christ as Lord and Savior. Jesus wants a lifelong partnership with us and has the same desire for married couples.

1. **First group.** Let us visit again Mark 10:9 "Therefore what God has joined together, let no one separate." The marriage concern seems to connect with verses 13–16 that deal with the children.[76] Both examples appear to fall into the same authoritative language. We share in Christ's lot, His God is our God, His Father is our Heavenly Father, and finally, Christ's glory is our glory. We therefore can only conclude that marriage was meant as a lifelong partner-

ship, just as God desires our partnership to be with Him. God blessed marriages, and no human being has the right to separate what God has joined together.

2. **Second group**. There is one question to ask ourselves when considering a divorce: "Was our marriage blessed by God or legally arranged by the court?" I contend that a court arrangement is only a secular function that is totally unrelated to the Christian function of marriage. We can easily say that God never blessed a marriage such as this. There is no scriptural support for that claim, but it is a consideration. It appears to me that there were no secular court marriages during the period when the Bible was written. The spirit of the Old and New Testament seems to support this logical conclusion.

3. **Third group**. The kingdom of God is also about God's grace, forgiveness and the reconciliation of Christian faith. All the pain that comes out of a divorce can end with God's forgiveness. God views divorce as one more result of sin. God loves us too much; He will never turn His back on people who are divorced. A reconciliation of that unfortunate suffering can occur. A repentant divorcee can be forgiven and can begin a new life with another partner in a marriage blessed by God. All partnerships exist for the glory of God. Therefore, all marriages that have a partnership also exist for the glory of God.

The Sociology of Divorce

Society either has a positive or negative impact on a family. The force of this impact is social pressure without the law of the land. These social pressures tend to invade the privacy of the family. The law of the land has no relevancy to a family's personal business. The positive or negative impact is relative to what the majority membership rules. Although there are two impacts, one soon learns that there are three choices to select from. Whether or not:

1. To allow the negative impact to punish one's bad decision.
2. To allow the positive impact to reward one's good decision.
3. To make an independent decision on a course of action that is neither negative nor positive.

The third point is a warning: Both the negative and positive are only relative to the majority rule of a society's membership, and one simply makes the personal decision that seems the most appropriate. This does not say that the majority is absolutely correct or wrong. A marriage is, therefore, not to be maintained solely on social pressures. A marriage blessed by God operates under the milieu of the "separation between church and state."

We have covered the generating principle that becomes the common thread in our fabric of sociological impacts on marriages. Counselors have tried to introduce facts about potential threats in a marriage, hoping their clients will make a positive decision. A family's solution is always unique and cannot be influenced by any social pressure with or without the laws of the land. The solution must remain private and appropriate only for that family.

Numerous married couples tend to avoid making the tough-love decision, which ultimately mends or breaks up a marriage.[††] They allow outsiders to make their decisions with irrelevant recommendations. An untrained outsider cannot fully understand other couples' problems. Although suggestions are offered by a close friend who might have deep concern and love for that couple's problems, there is always the potential mistake and the chance that the hurting couple might allow the friend's conclusion to become their only conclusion. Who can deny that the friend's suggestions are relative only to social pressures without the law of the land? Couples without the healthy state of mind to make appropriate decisions should seek a professional family counselor near their home.

A counselor will not make decisions for clients, but rather, as Aaron Rutledge wrote:

> If a marital diagnosis reveals that continued marriage of a couple not only promises nothing in the way of a healthy relationship, but points to marked personality destruction for one or both, it is the marriage counselor's responsibility to underline this prognosis. To be sure, one of the couple must make the decision to separate or not to separate, to divorce or not to divorce. But the counselor may be derelict in some cases unless he or she gives his/her opinion of the advisability of ending, with as little hurt as possible, a relationship that can bring only continued destruction of personality. (pp. 67–68).

Rutledge further underlines that the final decision of divorce or no divorce ultimately belongs to couples who are not obligated to continue their marriage at all cost.

Walter R. Stokes offered support to Rutledge, but with a slightly different slant: "I suspect that because marriage has been for so long entrenched as a religious sacrament, many marriage counselors still feel impelled to preserve marriage at all cost..." (p. 67). His primary focus is "upon the dignity and satisfactions of individual spouses and only secondarily upon the sociological values associated with the marriage." Again, the inference was relative to social pressures with or without the law of the land. These sociological values being interwoven in the fabric of social pressure tend to be fearfully all too subtle. A couple deserves freedom from this fearful addition to what is already a complex problem.

Wherein democracy provides all people the freedom of speech, assembly and worship, some moralists appear to forget about an equal freedom not to worship, taking or quitting a job, or especially asking for or denying divorce without the sociological values. All human freedoms do not negate irresponsible misuse, and divorce is certainly included. Irresponsible misuse of divorce can be cruel, exploitative and tragic. But, the responsible divorce can be humane, kind and spiritually freeing. Most people ought to receive an education on responsible marriage and divorce.

The primary focus for an education ought to be for couples with children. Children suffer emotional damage whether being separated from a parent (it is usually a separation from the father), or when parents remain married for the sake of their children. The choice comes down to two alternatives that will cause emotional damage in children. The physical separation of the family allows more opportunity for healing among all members. Children will have a chance to adjust to life without their father if parents avoid telling their children that something horrible has happened.

Although he is both a psychologist and the executive director of the Institute for Rational Living in New York City, Dr. Albert Ellis offers divorce only as an alternative and will further help a couple "get through the divorce without unnecessary feelings of bitterness, resentment, failure and guilt" (p. 115). He supports the concept that sociological values cannot be imposed upon a couple already irresponsibly misusing divorce.

We only spoke about a divorced mother with children, but what about unwed mothers? Unwed mothers may have a different lifestyle than divorced mothers, but the consequence of having a child after a loving relationship does not negate the problem. Unwed mothers experience a tragedy similar to being divorced. William J. Goode claims that there are similarities between a divorced mother and an unwed mother. First, men perceive these women as "easy sex prey." Secondly, both kinds of mothers will be forced to decide on the proper solution. We already considered the divorced mothers, but the "proper" solutions for the unwed mothers tend to be:

1. Abortion.
2. Affixing the responsibility to the former lover.
3. Keeping the child as a memory of the true father.

All three are not great solutions, but, at best, the second and third would better serve the mother than the first. Unwed mothers ought to seek a certified counselor for professional help, just like divorced mothers should. Homes for unwed mothers are also available in some cities.

The Psychology of Divorce

A mind can be easily influenced by damaging, fearful thoughts about divorce. Psychologists who offer the neutral-based counseling allow the divorced person to feel safe during the period of development, maintenance and restoration. Such a support can come from "Parents without

Partners" or the "SOS — Focus on Divorce." The following is a short list of their objectives:

1. Offer a more objective understanding of the causes of conflicts and a realistic look at the future.
2. Alleviate feelings of loneliness, guilt and the common failure of all couples.
3. Improve the attitudes and behaviors of parents that will help children through this troubled time. (p. 414)

Perhaps psychologists will ask clients to obtain books on the laws about divorce which both can discuss together. This is recommended, and here are three suggestions:

1. *Your Marriage and the Law.* (1952) Harriet Pilpel; T. Zavin.
2. *The Divorce Handbook.* (1960) F. Haussamen; M. A. Guitar.
3. *The Complete Guide to Divorce.* (1967) S. G. Kling.

We have not dealt much with the conflicts children experience prior, during and after their parents' divorce. Unless help is offered to children in the first stage, they too will grow up with an equal potential for conflicts in their marriage. Let us consider five developmental stages most commonly known among children with divorced parents:

1. Children experience the same hurt and emotional moods as their parents do during each conflict. Parents tend to avoid children and their questions.
2. Children grieve the separation from one parent after the divorce. Parents must avoid criticism of each other

and allow their children to choose sides for live-in and visitation rights. The children's shock and painful experiences from the divorce can be reduced and can receive by remaining in the same house, seeing the same neighbors, attending the same school and church, and following familiar routines.

3. Children experience confusion and guilt in loyalty to their separated parents. Promises of visitation dates ought to be kept. The non-absent parent should not insist that the reluctant older child should visit the absent parent, but rather allow the psychologist to discuss this with that child. The parent who has custody of the children ought not "pump" for information by asking "who, where, why and what," since this will erode the children's experience and violate their right to a private relationship with the absent parent.
4. Children will resent each parent who begins to date another person by such expressions as: insecurity via hitting, shoving, biting, kicking, pushing, tripping, and / or incessant whining and crying. Their adolescence can lash out to conflict with peers, adults and civil authorities. The psychologist ought to tell these children that their parents may have acted unwisely in some instances, but no one is perfect.
5. The second marriage only compounds children's conflicts by the intrusion of the stepparent and stepchildren, who become the enemy. (pp. 417–423)

Children need proper guidance while facing all the above problems in their lives. There are books that all parents need to read for more support. The following list should be helpful:

- *Children of Divorce.* Despert, J. L. New York, NY: Double day, 1962.
- *Family Disorganization in Contemporary Social Problems.* Goode, W. J.; Merton, R. K.; Nisbet, R. A. (eds). New York, NY; Harcourt, Bruce & World, 1966.
- *Children's Views of Themselves.* Washington, D.C.: Association for Children Education International, 1959.
- *Child Behavior.* Ilg, F. L.; Ames, L. B., New York, NY: Del Publishing Co., 1962.
- *"Seven Mistakes Divorced Parents Make"* Pollack, J. H. Parents Magazine, March, 1967 Issue, page 48 f.
- *The Social Context of Marriage.* Udry, J. R. New York, NY: Lippincott, J. B., 1966.

This concludes a look at psychological problems being caused by divorce. We basically learned how severe one's emotional fabric breaks down regardless of age. We also learned no one becomes a winner in divorced families.

Conclusion

We have learned that suffering and trusting are important ingredients for any solid partnership, such as with God or between married partners. All partnerships exist for the glory of God. Therefore, all marriages that have a partnership also exist for the glory of God. We also learned that a couple must decide to which group they belong:

- First group requires lifelong partnership in marriage and Christian life.
- Second group is a secular marriage officiated in a court and not blessed by God.
- Third group belongs in the kingdom of God, just as Jesus promises children.

The kingdom of God is about God's grace, forgiveness and reconciliation in a Christian's faith and marriage. Regardless of the decision, a couple must decide alone, with or without outside help from their society.

Addendum Seven

My Ministry as a Chaplain

My twenty-two-year ministry as a chaplain for the US Army reserve—over nine years of active duty and 12 years in two Veterans Affairs Medical Centers—includes a mixture of positive and negative experiences. One could say this should be no different than life itself. Those experiences served as a challenge to accept truth without fantasy. I only want to share my personal experiences to describe my ministry as a chaplain. My story should not be much different than the average chaplain and, therefore, represents the norm.

Introduction to the Chaplaincy

The Webster's Third New International Dictionary represents a fair definition for chaplain and the chaplaincy. I quote the following:

> Chaplain: 1. (a) clergyman /(woman) appointed to officiate in a chapel, (b) Church (...) Clergyman /(woman) without a title or benefice in the place where he/(she) officiates, who performs religious services in a Chapel, Cathedral, or collegiate church. 2: A clergyman /(woman) officially attached to the army or navy, to some public institution, or to a family or court. 3: Any person chosen to conduct religious exercises (as for a society). The Chaplaincy is the office, position, or station of a chaplain.

Although the armed forces require chaplains to wear the uniform representing each branch—Army, Navy or Air Force—we must be mindful that the Navy shares their chaplains with the Marine Corps. Webster concluded his definition with a brief description of a chaplain's duty: "To conduct religious exercises (as for a society)."

Qualifications

The qualifications will vary for military, hospital, prison and industry chaplains. A basic requirements include:

- Graduate of a recognized college with a bachelor degree.
- Graduate of a recognized seminary with a master's of divinity degree,
- Ministry for a minimum of three years in his/her own church.
- Must be endorsed by his / her own church.

Additional requirements usually consist of training that empowers adaptability to the given milieu of the institution, such as a clinical pastoral education for a hospital ministry. I recommend that all clergy should contact the institution that he or she has an interest in for a more definitive explanation. They eagerly await your inquiry.

Theology

The chaplaincy seeks to define God's calling for His chosen people by serving as His representative in a divine mission. His chosen servants must continuously remember their calling is for a divine purpose; some are known to have forgotten. A final theological message is in God's covenant with His servants; both God and His servants are committed to this divine mission.

The Divine Mission

The divine mission for chaplains is to facilitate a spiritual relationship between God and people. God and His servants will only offer an opportunity for people to accept or reject this spiritual relationship. A chaplain does not go beyond that juncture. Many people who are not associated with the chaplaincy find that restriction to be unacceptable. These people have the right to such an opinion and any chaplain honors that. This example of restriction is only one reason, among others, to protect another person's opinion.

Chaplains see people from many faith groups, and each group must receive appropriate respect for its theological beliefs. A chaplain is therefore well trained in the knowledge of these faith groups, and it becomes the resource that facilitates a relationship between God and His people.

The Purpose

The purpose of a chaplain is to fill the void between a person's on going spiritual life in a community church and their temporary institutional hospitalization. His /her pastor in that community seldom offers as much pastoral support as a chaplain offers to patients. A chaplain can fill that void of time. This explanation should help relate why there is such a restriction on the chaplain's mission. The mission assumes that each patient already has had quality time studying their church's theological / doctrinal teaching. A chaplain will make every possible effort to honor and respect this background. A chaplain simply facilitates a patient's belief system in order to fill the void of time. The primary purpose for a chaplain is to bring people to God and God to the people. One cannot find a more privileged reward than this divine purpose.

Weaknesses of the Chaplaincy

The weaknesses in the chaplaincy are most likely the same as any community (civilian) church. Clergies in the community are not only competing with one another, but people with no church affiliation are known to pass judgment on any religious organization. They only tolerate living near a church or near neighbors who attend church. Chaplains experience this kind of response. Since laws protect our freedom to worship and have our religious organizations, people without any church affiliation remain powerless. This could easily be one reason that these people are vindictive toward any government employment where there is a chaplaincy. This person without church affiliation could easily be a medical doctor, social worker or a respiratory therapist who is expected to support the chaplain. Resentment for this expectation of respect can overcome them. He or she feels powerful whenever he or she successfully uses the regulations as a convenient way to avoid chaplains.

Another weakness is the fact that no law, regulation or policy could be written to demand that religious activities be imposed on any person or group of people. Only the right for everyone to practice religious functions must be protected. The equation in military or federal regulations does not preclude vindictive people from manipulating these regulations for their convenience. It is nearly impossible to catch these people. Only their consciences can convict them of taking religious rights away from the deserving people who are prevented from seeing a chaplain and receiving any sacraments of prayer for the sick, communion or a worship service. Vindictive people to compromise a chaplain's mission can abuse regulations, policies and executive guidelines.

Competition exists between some chaplains, and I hardly believe that one could claim the same competition does not occur among civilian clergies. What causes this unfortunate display of behavior? A very common trend in military and federal government chaplaincies is for some chaplains to have low morals and ethics. What is a common trend among civilian clergies? Can we point at the two "Jimmys" for having low morals and ethics as well? Thank God we are not the judges of sin. All clergies must focus on the reality that low morals and ethics not only tend to damage positive images, but they are also not easily removed.

Military chaplains have rank, and I always found that this intimidated most soldiers. There are chaplains who enjoy having rank, and others, like myself, can still function without it. The only time I found rank to be helpful was in being able to talk with the commander without getting permission. An army tradition gives credence to this kind of action by chaplains. I somehow believe this same credence could be extended to chaplains without the need for rank. Perhaps the GS ratings, as used in the federal government, should be implemented as an acceptable system for military chaplains.

A common complaint among chaplains is the lack of social freedom. Chaplains are not always allowed to attend their church conferences or meet with the other clergy from their own church affiliation. As if this is not enough, their own church leadership seldom offers support by working out this problem with the military and federal government. There is no flexibility on either end to support chaplains who only want time off to attend these functions.

I recall a very popular question from staff members at the VA Medical Center, "Where do you attend church?" I tried to show why chaplains, along with their own pastors, could not conduct a ministry at the very same time other ministries are being conducted. A person's body cannot be at two locations at the same time. I also asked whether they could understand why their missionaries are not able to attend a local church. The answer was always, "Why, of course they can't." I rest my case.

Strengths in the Chaplaincy

Chaplains are God's chosen people who truly believe their work is to be a calling. They need nothing else to conquer evil. God is with chaplains, wherever that might be; and who could be against God? There will always be unhappiness, just as there will also be happiness in serving other people who need pastoral functions. God's power and glory will always get a chaplain through any problem.

Chaplains serve people where, otherwise, no spiritual support would be offered. Military chaplains serve in the most dangerous combat location, or wherever a soldier is sent on a mission. VA chaplains conduct sacraments at the intensive-care units, prior to surgery or whenever a patient requests spiritual support.

Chaplains receive training on all faith groups in order to understand the fundamentals of various theological preferences. This empowers a chaplain to facilitate spiritual growth in anyone's faith system.

All chaplains are highly educated in colleges, universities and seminaries. They are professionally trained in their particular field—military, hospital or prison ministry—and often receive up-dated skills through various schools and workshops. This was already mentioned in the qualifications section, but it is also relevant as one of the strength of the chaplaincy. It would be my guess that a chaplain in any field would have completed the equivalent of at least 135 extra semester hours of academic study beyond his /her degree during a career.

Chaplains are the only people who have the authority to conduct a worship service and offer sacraments to those who want them. They are also the only people who are requested during times of fatal crisis. Although many lay people could be mentioned for having done these services for people, and they ought to be commended with the deepest respect, only chaplains are fully trained. This accounts for the reason why chaplains are more accessible than any other group of professionals. An appointment is not always required to see a chaplain, but it is the case to see a doctor. A bill is not sent to the people involved after counseling, but lawyers and doctors do send one. A chaplain conducting a ministry on the street or in the halls of a hospital is a common sight. They are available twenty-four hours a day, seven days a week.

Clinical Pastoral Education

The Clinical Pastoral Education (CPE) program includes positive and negative elements. I cannot remember when it officially began, but I can say that my first unit was done in 1970. I noticed a lot of positive changes after that date. The program equips chaplains with the highly competitive skills necessary to offer patients outstanding pastoral care. I had a CPE supervisor on my staff, and together our chaplains and seminary students were taught well.

CPE prepares a person for the professional care of other people, and, indeed, it also enables a chaplain to better understand him or herself while being under incredible stress. Patients will be "ugly" and simply mean toward anyone, but the professional person must realize that this is common and the patient is not singling out one individual. This does not mean that all professionals are on guard against this kind of incident, but it does report what can cause this stress. A male nurse once shared how he would handle the problem: He takes off for one year doing whatever comes to mind. This one year away from the hospital always gave him back all the energy he needed to cope with hospital care.

Teamwork is very important among clinic professionals. Members of a team depend on each other's individual assessments of the patient. I recall a comment from one doctor who claimed that my assessment of a patient's five-year grief over the loss of his daughter became the doctor's reason to change medications. That comment began my new approach to writing patients' assessments. I made sure my comments were clinically correct and clearly understood. I often reminded my chaplains to write at least one intelligent sentence in the "Progress Notes."

A Chaplain's Typical Work Schedule

A US Army chaplain's schedule could be the following:

- 0600–0700 hours to take PT and three-mile run with troops.
- 0700–0800 hours clean up for work.
- 0800–1200 hours will be office work, counseling, staff meeting and area visitation—including hospital and stockade.
- 1200–1300 hours lunch.
- 1300–1800 hours (or later) As soon as the commander leaves, continue the same work as in the morning.
- 1700–0800 hours will be for on-call status (rotated).
- 1800 hours or later will be the evening meal.

This schedule varies depending on requests from the unit and whether or not the unit is in field training. The chaplain can be in the field for three weeks or longer. Four to ten counseling sessions could be scheduled each day. Meetings are also scheduled with the unit commander and the post chaplain. Chaplains have private discussions with the commander and his subordinates concerning any problem a soldier might have brought up. My last active-duty assignment included:

- Garrison chaplain to manage the chapel activities.
- Supervised the director of Christian education and the assistants.
- Responsible for a ministry that included two units, a hospital, a stockade and a Sunday school department.
- Four thousand retirees lived in the community.
- Manage an alternate chaplain for the Family Crisis Center when their chaplain took off.

The VA Medical Center requires chaplains to work eight hours a day, five days per week. All overnight callbacks to visit seriously ill patients or families of the deceased will be charged against the forty hours per week. The following was a typical daily schedule:

- Check new admissions, the seriously ill list and patient transfers.
- Check with the chief for his/her requirements or new important information.
- Conduct visitations, worship services, sacraments and attend ward staff meetings. The chief also conducts monthly meetings. Chaplains rotate leading Sunday morning worship service and being on call during the night. The chief's schedule becomes much more in volved and does not follow the eight-hour day. The chief attends all required executive meetings.
- Writes department policy and reports for the director, for quality assurance, safety and budget offices.
- Prepares staff evaluations.
- Responds to letters from outside.

Do Chaplains "Leave" the Ministry?

Some people may consider this question to be unusual, and I hope they would. Regardless, many sincere people who honestly have little or no idea what a chaplain does ask this question. All chaplains are ordained and endorsed by their church to represent that church. My primary claim is that chaplains *never* leave the ministry. They are in the mainstream of a ministry.

Still another honest question: How shall I address you after retirement? Again, there is very little difference from a pastor. One remains ordained and has all the rights and authority that were originally given. Titles such as *Rev.*, *Chaplain*, or *Pastor* remain valid. Army regulations require a chaplain to remain available for active duty until the age of 60 years, and, in my opinion, the title remains for a lifetime. The chaplain's endorsement by his/her church must be renewed periodically. The director of church and ministry service in Anderson, Indiana, is my endorsing agency.

Can a Chaplain Support the Community Church?

The problem of no flexibility was already introduced. You will recall that chaplains primarily serve the soldiers in the military, patients in the VA Medical Centers, and prisoners in the prisons. Regulations also limit the free time that a chaplain can support the community church. Consequently, there are only a few occasions when a chaplain has an opportunity for community support.

- During the local, state and national minister meetings.
- Participating in the local Good Friday, Easter and Veterans Day services.
- Occasionally attend a congregation just to remain in contact with that church.

My ministry as a chaplain was both fulfilling and a challenge for me. The greatest credit goes to our Lord who was with me always, even when everyone else might have questioned a particular action I might have taken. I now look forward toward the future.

Notes

† Genesis 17:7; 18:18; 22:17; Numbers 23:19; 1 Samuel 2:10, 35; Psalms 144:3; Isaiah 7:14; 9:6; Ezekiel 2:1–8; 3:1–4; Daniel 7:13–14; Micah 7:7.

†† The following data is based on a book entitled, *Handbook of Marriage Counseling*, Edited by Ben N. Ard, JR. and Constance C. Ard. Page number references follow all the quotations from this book for the duration of "The Sociology of Divorce."

1 Henry Bettenson. Editor, "Documents of the Christian Church." (Second Edition), London, Oxford University Press, New York, Toronto, 1963. pp. 71-116.

2 Gustavo Gutierrez. *A Theology of Liberation*. New York: Orbis Books, 1973, pp. 145–146.

3 *Teaching for Results*. Nashville, Tennessee, Broadman Press, 1956, pp. 30–31.

4 *The Divine-Human Encounter*. Philadelphia: Westminster Press, 1943, p. 85.

5 Clemmons, Robert S. *Dynamics of Christian Adult Education*. New York:Abingdon Press, 1966, pp. 123–24.

6 Editor of *Creative Procedures for Adult Groups*, N.Y.: Abingdon Press, 1968, pp. 27–32.

[7] *The Art of Teaching Christianity*. N.Y.: Abingdon Press, 1968, pp. 22–25.

[8] Paul Bergevin, Dwight Morris, and Robert M. Smith, *Adult Education Procedures*. Connecticut: The Leabury Press, 1963, p. 43.

[9] Ibid., p. 43.

[10] Romans 6:3–11; 2 Corinthians 5:17; Colossians 3:9–11.

[11] Leviticus 24:12; 1 Chronicles 28:9; Isaiah 26:3.

[12] Miller, Chuck. *Youth Evangelism*. Spring issue, 1969, p. 6.

[13] Romans 1:17; Galatians 3:11; Hebrews 10:38.

[14] Romans 6:8; 1 Timothy 1:16; 2 Timothy 1:12

* Webster's Third New International Dictionary of the English Language Unabridge: "Our Use of Love" Editor in Chief Philip Babcock Gove, Ph.D G.&C. Merriam Company, Publisher Springfield, Massachusetts, USA page 1340

[15] Heschel, Abraham J., *The Prophets: An Introduction*. Harper Torchbooks, 1969, p. 39.

[16] Hailey, Homer. *A Commentary on the Minor Prophets*, Baker Book House, Grand Rapids, MI., 1972, p. 186.

[17] Ibid., p. 222.

[18] Ibid., p. 225.

[19] Psalms 49:6–7 on limitation; Proverbs 18:11; 28:11 on trusting too much of self; Job 21 and Jeremiah 12 on transitory character; Luke 12:16–21 and Matthew 19:23 on wrong selfish interests and imperiling salvation; 1 Timothy 6:17 is on high-minded foolishness.

[20] *A Commentary on the Minor Prophets*, p. 248., Ibid, p. 271

[21] Ladd, George Edlon. *The Theory of the New Testament: Part I & II, The Gospel*. Class Lectures of Dr. Ladd, 1967. page V-9.

[22] Ladd, George Eldon. *EQ*, 30, 1958, p. 140.

[23] Isaiah 7:13 ff.; 9:6 f.; 11:1 ff.; Jeremiah 23:5 f.; 33:14 ff.; Micah 5:2 ff.

[24] Matthew 12:28; Mark 1:15; Luke 11:20.

[25] Baker's Dictionary of Theology; p. 190.

[26] Ibid., p. 189.

[27] Matthew 9:32–34; 11:7–19; 12:15–32; Luke 7:24–35; Mark 5:1–20.

[28] Walvoord, John F. *Daniel: The Key to Prophetic Revelation*. p. 268.

[29] Box, G. H. *The People and the Book*. 1925, p. 453.

[30] cf. E.J. Young, *The Prophecy of Daniel*, 1949, pp. 154 ff.; G. Vos, *Self Disclosure*, pp. 44 ff.; and Reisenfeld in *The Background of the N.T.*, p. 87.

[31] John 5:42, 10:27, 13:18; Acts 16:14; 1 Corinthians 14:25.

[32] Deuteronomy 9:6–7; 1 Chronicles 28:19; Mark 13:14; 1 Corinthians 12:1–3; Philippians 1:12–14; etc.

[33] Exodus 23:1–3; Deuteronomy 5:20; Ezekiel 21:23; Matthew 5:11–12; Acts 6:8–15.

[34] Matthew 22:36–38; John 7:38; Acts 11:21; Romans 10:9.

[35] Matthew 16:18; Ephesians 5:21–24; Colossians 1:18; Revelation 1:4, 11, 20.

[36] Matthew 9:36; 25:32; 26:31; Mark 6:34; 14:27; John 10:2–16; Hebrews 13:20; 1 Peter 2:25; 5:4.

[37] Matthew 13:11; Luke 8:10; 1 Corinthians 4:1; 13:2; 14:2.

[38] Genesis 6:4; Hosea 1:10; John 1:12; 1 John 3:1.

[39] Jeremiah 1:4–10; Mark 1:20; Luke 10:1–12.

[40] William Barclay's commentary: *The Gospel of Matthew: Volume 1*; p. 396.

[41] Ibid., p. 397.

[42] Ibid., p. 398.

[43] Paragraph summarized: ibid., p. 398. Everett F. Harrison, editor-in-chief. *Baker's Dictionary of Theology*. "Annihilationism," pp. 43–44; "Immortality," pp. 280– 281.

[44] William Barclay, p. 400.

[45] A small, wingless, flattened insect that sucks blood. William Barclay, p. 401.

[46] William Barclay, p. 403.

[47] Ibid., pp. 403–404.

[48] Ibid., p. 404.

[49] Ibid., p. 410.

[50] Isaiah 9:1–4; Matthew 4:12–23; 1 Corinthians 1:10–17.

[51] Matthew 16:18; Ephesians 5:23; Colossians 1:18.

[52] Romans 1:17; Galatians 3:11; Hebrews 10:38.

[53] Romans 6:8; 1 Timothy 1:16; 2 Timothy 1:12.

[54] Matthew 28:19; Acts 2:32–33; 1 Corinthians 12:3–6; 2 Corinthians 13:13.

[55] Galatians 3:26; 4:1–7, 31; 5:1–6; 6:1–10; Ephesians 2:4.

[56] John 1:41; Acts 10:38; Romans 9:5.

[57] Genesis 32:32; 45:21; 46:8; Exodus 1:9; 2:23,25.

[58] Romans 6:8; 1 Timothy 1:16; 2 Timothy 1:12.

[59] Matthew 4:1–11; Mark 1:21–34; Luke 2:41–52; John 17:25–26.

[60] Matthew 8:14, 23–27; 14:13–21; John 11:38–44, 19:26; Acts 2:1–13, 9:36–43, 12:6–19.

[61] Matthew 7:21; Mark 2:28, 8:29; John 20:28, 21:7.

[62] Leviticus 5:5; Philippians 2:11; James 5:16.

[63] Mark 2:18–20; John 10:11–18, 17:6–19.

[64] Leviticus 19:18; Matthew 5:43; 19:19; 22:39; Mark 12:31–33; Romans 13:9b; Galatians 5:14; 1 Thessalonians 4:9; James 2:8.

[65] Deuteronomy 6:5; Mark 12:30–33; Luke 10:27.

[66] *Strong's Exhaustive Concordance of the Bible*, pp. 29–30; and the *Concordance to the Greek*, Westcott and Hort, Tischendorf, pp. 230–1.

[67] *Strong's*, p. 24; *Concordance to the Greek*, p. 231).

[68] *Strong's*, p. 30; *Concordance to the Greek*, p. 347; Arndt, William F., Gingrich, F. W. *Greek-English Lexicon of the New Testament*, p. 278.

[69] Matthew 28:18; Luke 24:49; Acts 1:7; 2:4.

[70] California: Regal Books Division, G/L Publication, 1972, p. 35.

[71] God's power: Matthew 6:13; 26:64; Mark 9:1. God issues power: Luke 1:35; 5:17; John 1:12; Acts 1:8; 4:7; 6:8; 8:19; Romans 15:13; Colossians 1:11.

[72] 2 Corinthians 4:7; Romans 2:29; Revelation 19:1.

[73] Romans 8:28; 9:11, 17; Ephesians 3:7–13; 1 John 3:7–10.

[74] Baker's dictionary of theology, page 169 Everett F. Harrison, editor in chief: cf. Leviticus 21:7, 14; 22:13; Numbers 30:9; Deuteronomy 22:19, 29; Isaiah 50:1; Jeremiah 3:1; Ezekiel 44:22.

[75] Matthew 5:32b; 19:9; Mark 10:11–12; Luke 16:18.

[76] Supported by *The Cambridge Greek Testament Commentary*: C.F.D. Moule, general editor, and C.E.B. Cranfield, Author of *St. Mark Commentary*, p. 322.

Bibliography

Alves, Rubem A. *A Theology of Human Hope.* Indiana: Abbey Press, 1975.

Bergevin, Paul; Morris, Dwight; Smith, Robert M. *Adult Education Procedures.* Connecticut: The Leabury Press, 1963.

Brunner, Emil. *The Divine-Human Encounter.* Philadelphia: Westminster Press, 1943.

Bruner, Frederick Dale. *A Theology of the Holy Spirit.* Grand Rapids, Michigan: William B. Eerdmans / Publisher, 1976.

Clemmons, Robert S. *Dynamics of Christian Adult Education.* New York: Abingdon Press, 1966.

Cone, James H. *Liberation.* Philadelphia & New York: J.B. Lippincott Co., 1970.

Cone, James H. *A Black Theology of Liberation.* Philadelphia & New York: J.B. Lippincott Co., 1970.

Edge, Findley B. *Teaching for Results.* Nashville, TN., Broadman Press, 1956.

Erikson, Erik H. *Childhood and Society.* New York: W.W. Norton & Co., Inc., 1963.

Fanon, Frantz. *The Wretched of the Earth.* New York: Grove Press, Inc., 1968.

Fitch, William. *The Ministry of the Holy Spirit.* Grand Rapids, Michigan: Zondervan Publishing House, 1974.

Freire, Paulo. *Pedagogy of the Oppressed.* New York: The Seabury Press, 1970.

Gutierrez, Gustavo. *A Theology of Liberation.* New York: Orbis Books, 1973.

Haley, Alex. *Roots.* New York: Doubleday & Co., Inc., 1976.

Hendry, George S. *The Holy Spirit in Christian Theology.* Philadelphia: The Westminster Press, 1956.

Holt, John. *How Children Fail.* New York: Dell Publishing Co., Inc., 1973.

———. *How Children Learn.* New York: Dell Publishing Co., Inc., 1973.

Jewett, Paul K. *Man as Male and Female.* Michigan: William B. Eerdmans Publishing Co., 1976.

Kilgore, James. *Being a Man in a Woman's World.* California: Harvest House Publishers, 1975.

Koenig, Robert E. *Christian Education: Shared Approaches.* Philadelphia: United Church Press, 1975.

Ladd, George Eldon. *Jesus and the Kingdom: The Eschatology of Biblical Realism.* New York, Evanston & London: Harper & Row, Publishers, 1964.

———. *The Theolgy of the New Testament: Part I & II, The Gospels.* Class Lectures of Dr. Ladd, 1967.

Lehmann, Paul L. *Ethics in a Christian Context.* New York & Evanston: Harper & Row, Publishers, 1963.

Malcolm X; Haley, Alex. *The Autobiography of Malcolm X.* New York: Grove Press, Inc., 1966.

Memmi, Albert. *The Colonizer and the Colonized.* New York: The Orin Press, 1965.

Minor, Harlold D., ed. *Creative Procedures for Adult Groups.* N.Y.: Abingdon Press, 1968.

Murray, John Courtney S.J. *The Problem of Religious Freedom.* Westminster, Maryland: The Newman Press, 1965.

Nelson, Ellis C. *Where Faith Begins.* Atlanta: John Knox Press, 1971.

Reist, Benjamin A. *Beyond Ideological Theology* (From McKelway, A.J. and Willis, E. David, Context of Contemporary Theology). Atlanta: John Knox Press, 1974.

Rood, Wayne R. *The Art of Teaching Christianity.* N.Y.: Abingdon Press, 1968.

Rowbothan, Sheila. *Woman's Consciousness, Man's World.* Maryland: Penguin Books, 1976.

Skinner, Tom. *Black and Free.* New York: New Family Library, 1972.

Taylor, Marvin J., ed. *Foundation for Christian Education in an Era of Change.* Nashville: Abingdon, 1976.

Tillich, Paul. *Systematic Theology: Volume III.* Chicago: The University of Chicago Press, 1963.

Turner, Charles Hampden. *Radical Man.* New York: Anchor Books. Doubleday & Co., Inc., 1971.

ARTICLES

Army Regulations 600-30. "Human Self-Development Program." HQ, Department of the Army, October, 1971.

Cone, James H. "Black Theology and Reconciliation," Christianity and Crisis. XXXII (January 22, 1973).

Field Manual 21-6. "Military Training." HQ, Department of the Army, No. 1975.

Kim, Chi Ha. "To All Who Cherish Justice and Truth." Princeton Theological Seminary Library, Reserved Shelf—Copied.

From Princeton Theological Seminary Religious Reading Room:

Rugg, H. "Imagination."

Moran, Bagriel. "The Time for a Theology."

Prenter, Regin. "Spiritus Creator."

Ramsey, Ivan. "Christian Education," "Religious Language."

Wyckoff, D. Campbell. "Understanding Your Church Curriculum."

To order additional copies of

A Liberating Life from Silence

have your credit card ready and call

1 (800) 917-BOOK

or send $13.95 + $3.99 shipping and handling to

WinePress Publishing
PO Box 1406
Mukilteo, WA 98275

www.winepresspub.com